In the online economy today, entrepreneurs and users alike need better options—and this is a great place to start. Boyd Cohen has created an essential roadmap for how real-world enterprises can discover opportunities the VCs won't tell them about.

Nathan Schneider, University of Colorado Scholar in Residence, Co-Founder Platform Cooperativism

Business as usual? Not necessarily! Boyd Cohen shows us how alternative business are quickly making their way to become the new normal.

Javier Creus, Founder, Ideas for Change

We live in oxymoronic times. On the one hand, market capitalism seems stuck in a planet-destroying groove where a general rising tide of wealth is not lifting all boats. On the other, we are seeing a new plural flourishing of energy, innovation, and social entrepreneurship. *Post-Capitalist Entrepreneurship* by Boyd Cohen, makes the compelling case that we are in a moment of transition and that the next wave entrepreneurship can be at the vanguard and foreshadow a more just, greener, and distributed post-capitalist economy.

The book picks up on the buzzy range of alternative forms of organizing in a post-capitalist economy, and highlights the role of the next entrepreneurs in accelerating that. In this, through a range of fascinating case studies and working examples, the ideas are brought to life and brings with it an abiding optimism and positivism. In a world with much pain and angst, this book does the reader a service. Whilst not ignoring the perils, it serves to direct our gaze onto the good that is here right now, and then some - it stretches us to imagine what could be.

Neil McInroy, CEO, Centre for Local Economic Strategies (CLES)

Boyd Cohen does a great job at mixing and at the same time clearly categorizing emergent new business and new entrepreneurial behaviours based on technology developments shaped by XXIst century ethics (platforms, DAOs, alternative finances, etc.).

A very necessary, timely, and optimist look at a post-capitalism future balancing what's technically feasible with what's socially desirable.

Albert Cañuigueral, Ouishare Spain

If our economies are to become sustainable and ethical, new forms of innovation and entrepreneurship will be central to the transformation. In this book, leading entrepreneurship scholar Boyd Cohen eloquently sets out valuable examples and important advice for city authorities facing up to the challenges involved.

Duncan McLaren, Author, *Sharing Cities*

By deeply understanding emerging technology and socioeconomics and being a world leader in the sharing economy movement, Boyd has produced a groundbreaking view on this emerging paradigm. It is critical we all start thinking about its implications in order, and we can shape a better world before the opportunity runs away from us.

Jamie Burke, Founder, Outlier Ventures

We can't continue to live with extractive forms of entrepreneurship that contribute to the ecological weakening of our planet and dangerous social inequalities, but just as importantly we can't live without new forms of 'generative' entrepreneurship that work with natural and human commons and communities, and create livelihoods for everyone. This shift is the subject of this important book, which asks, based on extensive documentation from the new actors themselves: What new forms of business do we need for this era of transition? Boyd Cohen is providing us a great service by guiding us through the new forms we need. For the young people seeking to construct a sustainable and fair future, this is a must.

Michel Bauwens, Director and Founder, P2P Foundation

A different type of innovation is possible - and desirable. One that doesn't rely on VC and proprietary assets to produce value for the few. In this book, Boyd Cohen accurately reveals a new paradigm for entrepreneurship that harnesses the potential of new technologies to nurture commons, fosters innovation at the grassroots level, and produces abundance. By shedding light on new approaches and opportunities, this book can inspire entrepreneurs to adopt more contributive models to address social, economic, and environmental challenges at scale.

Mara Balestrini, Research Director at Ideas for Change and Project Manager at Fab Lab Barcelona

In this book, business professor Boyd Cohen proposes ways of thinking and acting differently: He combines open innovation, open data, and alternative currencies, the platform co-op model, and blockchain technologies to frame a new imaginary for a post-capitalist economy. Required reading.

Trebor Scholz, Associate Professor for Culture & Media, The New School and Co-founder, Platform Cooperativism

Post-Capitalist Entrepreneurship by Boyd Cohen makes the compelling case that we are in a moment of transition and that the next wave entrepreneurship can be at the vanguard and foreshadow a more just, greener, and distributed post-capitalist economy.

Neil McInroy, CEO, Centre for Local Economic Strategies (CLES)

Post-Capitalist Entrepreneurship

Startups for the 99%

Boyd Cohen, PhD
EADA Business School
Universitat de Vic

CRC Press
Taylor & Francis Group
Boca Raton London New York

CRC Press is an imprint of the
Taylor & Francis Group, an **Informa** business
A PRODUCTIVITY PRESS BOOK

CRC Press
Taylor & Francis Group
6000 Broken Sound Parkway NW, Suite 300
Boca Raton, FL 33487-2742

Printed on acid-free paper

International Standard Book Number-13: 978-1-138-71339-0 (Hardback)

Library of Congress Cataloging-in-Publication Data

Names: Cohen, Boyd, author.
Title: Post-capitalist entrepreneurship : startups for the 99% / Boyd Cohen.
Description: Boca Raton, FL : CRC Press, [2018] | Includes index.
Identifiers: LCCN 2017017499 | ISBN 9781138713390 (hardback : alk. paper)
Subjects: LCSH: Social entrepreneurship.
Classification: LCC HD60 .C577 2018 | DDC 338/.04--dc23
LC record available at https://lccn.loc.gov/2017017499

**Visit the Taylor & Francis Web site at
http://www.taylorandfrancis.com**

**and the CRC Press Web site at
http://www.crcpress.com**

Printed and bound in the United States of America by
Edwards Brothers Malloy on sustainably sourced paper

I dedicate this book to my family and especially my children as I am keen to help discover an alternative path of prosperity for my son Mateo, daughter Ayla, and the billions of other children facing a much different future than the one I faced as a child.

Contents

Preface

After working for 3 years with Accenture, I decided to pursue a PhD in entrepreneurship and ended up at the University of Colorado. In the 15 plus years that have passed since I completed my PhD, my research and observations of entrepreneurial ecosystems have evolved substantially. I believe the world of innovation and entrepreneurship is evolving in very profound ways, which change a lot of our underlying assumptions about entrepreneurship. In my last book, *The Emergence of the Urban Entrepreneur*, I leveraged insights from several research projects, and my own experiences living and participating in entrepreneurial ecosystems throughout Europe and the Americas, to demonstrate that entrepreneurship is urbanizing. In the same book, I introduce the Urbanpreneur Spiral, which highlights how urbanization, collaboration, and democratization are transforming the entrepreneurial phenomenon in important ways.

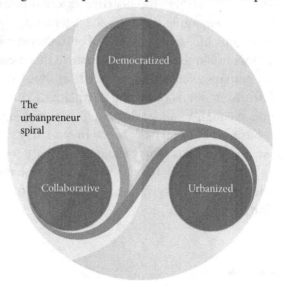

Through my research into topics such as the sharing economy, platform cooperatives, alternative currencies, and blockchain startups since the publication of *The Urban Entrepreneur*, I have come to realize that we are experiencing a profound change in the dynamics of startups. This includes the decreasing importance of and reliance on venture capital as a critical part of entrepreneurship. Also, the notion that entrepreneurs are driven by profit motive, seeking to scale venture-capital-backed companies until they can have a big payday, a multimillion dollar, or even a billion-dollar exit is giving way to something different. The 99% movement following the Great Recession demonstrated that many in society are frustrated by the growing inequalities and environmental impacts caused, at least in part, by the exploitation of companies supported by governments and lobbyists.

This book is based on evidence from my ongoing research and interactions with entrepreneurial communities, as well as my growing understanding of the drive toward a more distributed, "post capitalist" society, that entrepreneurship is changing and that the 99% are starting to rise up to challenge our notions of innovation, entrepreneurship, and capitalism itself. In summary, this book is dedicated to exploring the world of entrepreneurship beyond traditional thinking about monetization strategies, venture capital, scaling, growth hacking, and exits.

While my first book, with Hunter Lovins, *Climate Capitalism*, reflected my own belief that capitalism could be re-oriented to solve climate change, this book is an acceptance on my part that capitalism has failed to sufficiently resolve the negative externalities on communities and ecosystems emerging from the short-termism that has taken over much of economic life. As a professor of entrepreneurship in a private business school in Barcelona, EADA, I realize this message may be unexpected and perhaps even sound hypocritical. But I can no longer overlook the disturbing trends regarding technological unemployment, growing income inequality, and growing, not shrinking, ecological challenges that business as usual has created in our society. Yet, I am an eternal optimist, and this book aims to help show a path toward a better future, starting with entrepreneurs who are already reshaping markets and communities in ways that give me hope that the future could be much better than the present.

MARKET-BASED CAPITALISM DOES NOT EQUAL PROSPERITY!

"...there are broader questions to be asked about the efficacy of capitalism."

This quote did not come from Bernie Sanders or Thomas Piketty but rather from Goldman Sachs in a newsletter to investors in early 2016.

There is a growing recognition across the political spectrum in the United States and around the globe that capitalism as it is currently constructed is not functioning in a way that lifts all boats. Instead, the data suggest that the rich are getting richer, while income inequality, social unrest, and ecological challenges, such as declining biodiversity, deforestation, and climate change, are getting worse as a result of short-termism encouraged in neoliberal interpretations of capitalism. With this book, I do not intend to join the number of scholars and thought leaders who have been alerting us to the problems capitalism has been facing or causing, especially, but not exclusively, because of the changing dynamics of technology, jobs, and inequality. Many in recent years, such as Paul Mason, Doug Rushkoff, and Thomas Piketty, have covered this topic in ways that I never could. Instead, this book seeks to uncover emerging trends in entrepreneurship in a postcapitalist society that seeks to have more balance between society, nature, and the economy.

In recent years, we have witnessed an amazing amount of innovation and entrepreneurship that is inconsistent with the generally accepted principles of capitalism. While capitalism thrives on the concept of scarcity and how firms can monetize scarcity through intellectual property or ownership of finite resources and even labor, postcapitalism operates more on the concept of abundance. So, entrepreneurs embracing topics such as open innovation, open data, the commons, cooperative business models, alternative currencies, and emerging technology-enabled open-source organizations, such as distributed autonomous organizations (DAOs), are beginning to illustrate an alternative path forward for entrepreneurs wishing to change the relationship between economic activity and society. We could refer to this model as Open *Entrepreneurship*.

Even the widespread adoption of the lean startup methodology contributes to a shift in thinking because in most business schools where I have been in the past 15 plus years, aspiring entrepreneurs have been encouraged to write lengthy business plans detailing their unique competitive advantages, how they intend to protect and monetize them, and their path for obtaining multiple rounds of venture capital in order to gain near monopoly advantages. This is classical neoliberal capitalism at its best. While the lean startup method is being employed for these more classical approaches to entrepreneurship, lean startup also enables more members of society to participate in entrepreneurship without having exclusive or easy access to scarce resources. All of the aforementioned trends in entrepreneurship, which I have been researching for the past five years, lay the foundations for a reimagining of entrepreneurship beyond the 1%. This book aims to illustrate with concepts and real examples how entrepreneurship can thrive in a postcapitalist society and how the tools of innovation and entrepreneurship are being democratized so that the majority of society can participate in entrepreneurial activity in an age of abundance.

DRIVERS FOR THE NEED TO REIMAGINE ENTREPRENEURSHIP

The Occupy Movement with the "We Are the 99%" slogan, emerged as a reaction to a perception that the market-based form of capitalism employed in the United States, and to differing degrees in democracies around the globe, is beyond broken. The average citizen has grown increasingly convinced that the system is set up to help the rich get richer. Data on income inequality, such as the Gini Index, suggest that the public perception may be an accurate one. The 8 richest people in the world have the same aggregate wealth as the poorest 50% of the global population (i.e., 3.5 billion or so)! We have witnessed a decoupling of GDP growth and job growth in developed countries around the world. As companies have rebounded from the Great Recession, they have done so through increased automation and the use of temporary, freelance workers.

The printing press, steam engine, telephone, and the personal computer were all disruptive innovations, which brought not only more efficiency to markets but also generally speaking improved quality of life, wages, and employment levels. In the past few years, we have seen an explosion of thought leaders and academics suggesting that this phase of technology disruption we are witnessing is unlike those we witnessed, which contributed to the industrial revolution and the early stages of the digital revolution. One book which contributed to the growing recognition that something is different about the disruptive period we are living through now was *Race Against the Machine* by Erik Brynjolfsson and Andrew McAfee. Highlighting the growing power of technologies such as artificial intelligence (AI), big data, and automation, they demonstrated a convincing argument that the infinitely scalable technologies emerging today do not follow the same dynamics associated with prior technology innovations.

As such, we are witnessing a "great decoupling" of productivity gains and well-being. While companies are able to gain more efficiency and profits, they are doing so with fewer employees and paying them less for their services.

Until the 1980s, there was as a very strong correlation between increased productivity, GDP, and job and income growth. Yet, around the time the Internet emerged, we started witnessing a decoupling of these constructs. While companies may continue to reap the rewards of productivity-enhancing technologies, the middle and lower classes of society are actually witnessing a decline in jobs and income. As Andy Stern, the former head of SEIU, the largest labor union in the United States, highlighted in *Raising the Floor*, the decoupling has also been, not coincidentally, accompanied by a precipitous decline in union membership and strength in the United States and around the globe.

When I discuss the emerging technological unemployment with my research colleagues, some discount it as a fallacy of technological determinism. I argue that the data refute such arguments. We are clearly witnessing a new economic animal. And this is not only an issue for highly advanced economies. Asia has commonly been viewed as the factory of the West. Attracted by low wages, US and European companies migrated manufacturing in mass to Asian countries over the past few decades. Of course, this was the main critique by Donald Trump helping him to rise to the Presidency of the United States.

Yet, there are those who buy this argument that the US and European economies would thrive more if only companies were not allowed to outsource manufacturing to low-cost countries. As labor costs have steadily risen in China, companies started shifting their operations to lower-cost countries like Indonesia and Vietnam. However, as wages in those countries started increasing, companies began automating factories, and it was more cost-effective to automate than to employ and pay benefits to workers in those countries. A recent report by the International Labour Organisation (ILO) projects that up to 90% of garment and footwear workers in Cambodia and Vietnam are at risk of losing their jobs due to factory automation. Meanwhile, Foxconn, the major manufacturer for Apple in China, eliminated 60,000 jobs in just one factory due to the introduction of robotics.

So, could Trump have a point in encouraging Apple and other major US companies to produce more domestically? The evidence suggests that if the goal of this is to increase jobs and address income inequality, Trump and the US electorate who voted for him will be very disappointed.

In 2015, Adidas tested a new automated process in a new type of facility in Germany, which they refer to as a Speedfactory. It worked so well that Adidas announced plans for a Speedfactory soon in Western Europe. If Apple does indeed bring back manufacturing to the United States, you can bet they will do so in their own version of a Speedfactory, employing very few US citizens, just as Amazon has done with their highly automated distribution warehouses.

Okay, so if Asian factory workers will eventually lose out to automation, and American and European workers already have lost the battle against technology, then perhaps the hope for jobs in the Western world must rest with highly educated professionals who certainly cannot lose to technology, or could they? The World Economic Forum recently reported that over the next decade, 47% of all occupations could be affected by automation. As Stern highlighted in his book, no one is really safe from the technology disruptions we are witnessing. 3D printing is allowing more construction to occur with printers and robots in warehouses for later assembly on site, resulting in fewer construction workers and foremen. Big data is allowing for a growing amount of analytics work to be automated, leading to insights and fewer executives and managers. In early 2017, Goldman Sachs swapped out 600 traders for 200 programmers, aiming to further automate this white collar work.

In recent years, we have seen a growth in calls for a new economic model, which some refer to as postcapitalism. Proponents of a postcapitalist society see a need for greater changes. Rushkoff, in *Throwing Rocks at the Google Bus*, for example, explored how the knowledge society is not leading to greater income distribution and the rising of all boats but is actually exacerbating the wealth accumulation in the hands of the 1%. Both Rushkoff and Mason in *Postcapitalism* lament the emergence of mega platform digital peer-to-peer (P2P) "monopolies," like Airbnb and Uber, which seek global domination at all costs, arguing that P2P platforms owned by ambitious, venture-capital-backed corporations do not necessarily lead to further equality and amount to what Neal Gorenflo, my colleague and founder of Shareable, calls "platform deathstars."

Yet, Rushkoff refuses to actually blame executives and investors in Silicon Valley for the crisis of capitalism. Instead, he argues that they "are themselves caught up in a winner-takes-all race for dominance against all other digital behemoths. It's grow or die (pp. 3–4)."

We have also witnessed political upheaval around the globe, from the anti-austerity movement in Greece to Brexit in the United Kingdom and to Donald Trump becoming President of the United States. While some of these candidates and movements are left of the political spectrum, some come from the right, for me, at their core, they represent a growing discontent of the masses with the status quo. Citizens around the world are fed up with politics as usual, corruption, and perceived ills caused by globalization and immigration. Perhaps, most importantly, the people of the world are upset with declining wages, jobless growth, and net declines in real wages while companies and their shareholders seem to get richer.

The *financialization* of the world's markets, where a growing percentage of GDP is attributed to the financial sector through loans, insurance, derivatives, investment, and the like, has been steadily increasing for decades. As Mason reports in *Postcapitalism*, the financial sector in the United States increased its percentage of the GDP from 15% in the 1980s to about 25% in the early 2000s. So the bankers, stockbrokers, and investors are getting richer while the 99% are losing jobs to technology, particularly automation, commonly referred to as Industry 4.0.

INDUSTRY 4.0

Industry 4.0 has gained major traction in recent years. Driven by big data, the Internet of Things (IoT), artificial intelligence (AI), and robotics, companies are increasingly investing in automation technologies that will enable them to continue to increase efficiencies, and profits, without hiring new employees.

As I was writing this chapter, Amazon launched a new pilot project to develop mini grocery stores with zero cash registers (and no cashiers) using sensors and software to track what consumers take off the shelves and charge them automatically upon leaving the store. Automation is affecting high-tech industries, service industries, those of us in the developed world, and those in the developing world who hoped for stable work as part of the factory for the West.

A growing number of books have been written about these trends driving our thinking of postcapitalism, and many of those books contributed to my own thinking for this book. *Capital in the Twenty-First Century* by Piketty, *Postcapitalism* by Paul Mason, *Throwing Rocks at the Google Bus* by Douglass Rushkoff, and *Raising the Floor*, about the failure of the US economy to create sustained job growth and the potential transformational effect of a universal basic income (UBI) in the United States by

Andy Stern, all contributed to my understanding of the trends leading to the need to rethink our views on neoliberal market-based capitalism.

At least a scholar and author like myself is safe, right? Think again. Programmers, leveraging AI in Japan, recently were able to produce a short story for a literary competition, which advanced to the finals of the competition with a panel of judges who were completely unaware that the author was not a human but, in fact, a software program. Don't get me wrong. I love technology. And I believe much of the technological innovations we are witnessing are for the most part beneficial to humanity. But these innovations are not so good for people who want to actually work for a living in the future.

There are some, such as Wired's Kevin Kelly who, in *The Inevitable*, argue that AI will work to automate specific, more repetitive-type tasks, but just like the industrial revolution, will create even more jobs to complement AI. I don't believe this to be the case for most industries. Take autonomous cars, for example. Once our taxi fleets are fully autonomous, there will be little need for taxi drivers to do other related tasks. Sure, they might be able to reinvent themselves and find jobs in other fields or maybe 1% of taxi drivers will find work in helping to improve AI for taxi fleets, but the majority will be out of a job. Even if you look at more highly skilled professions, say a surgeon, I think you will not find more jobs for surgeons once AI allows for better diagnosis, more precision in determining the incision point, and, coupled with robotics, more precise operations with virtually zero risk for machine error. Sure, some surgeons will remain in employment helping the AI and robot and more may be employed (at least in the beginning) to improve the efficiency and accuracy of the technology. But, I am convinced, as are many others such as Andy Stern, that AI, automation, big data, and other emerging technologies will continue to decouple improved productivity and employment and income growth for the 99%.

This of course is one reason why I would like to turn my attention to entrepreneurship in a postcapital society as I believe it may be one of the few options remaining for those inclined to work.

FREELANCING AND THE GIG ECONOMY

As the trends discussed above suggest, full-time jobs with benefits will be increasingly rare in the coming decades. I have a friend in Barcelona with a 17-year-old daughter who is only interested in soft skills. My friend, Boris, is very concerned about what kind of economic future she will face, given the employment trends we are seeing and the unlikelihood his daughter will be able to contribute on the technology side of the disruptions we are facing. One bright spot I have shared with him is that even for those with full-time employment opportunities, there is growing interest, and I believe opportunity, for independent work.

In the United States, more than one in three working Americans are actively involved in independent freelancing activities. Researchers estimate that by 2020 or so, half of the US and European work force will be engaged in some form of independent work. True, much of this is driven by a lack of full-time employment opportunities for people. But that is only part of the story. A growing number of people entering the "work force" actually prefer the flexibility and variety and challenge of independent work. A recent survey by PWC found that 86% of respondents expressed a desire to work independently in the future because of greater flexibility in schedule and control over work environment, the opportunity to earn more, and a better work-life balance.* Technology-enabled freelancing, often referred to as the gig economy, is going to grow substantially in the future. Of course, there has been plenty of criticism about the early gig economy models, especially with Uber drivers. While some freelancers and gig economy members will be truly acting as independent entrepreneurs gaining those sought after advantages of an independent lifestyle, Uber drivers are not benefitting so much.

On the first day of my entrepreneurship courses to MBA students, I start with a series of questions to the class regarding different activities entrepreneurs engage in. I show them the picture of a local kiosk owner and ask if he is an entrepreneur or not. Inevitably, some say yes because he has invested his own money, runs his own business, and has no boss among other things. Others say no because there is no innovation in most kiosk businesses. I then start putting all of these characteristics like innovation, personal investment, and autonomy on a whiteboard so that we can have a broader discussion of the different dimensions of entrepreneurship, illustrating that most things in entrepreneurship are gray and not black and white. I then show the video of a woman who bought the rights to a McDonald's franchise. Is she an entrepreneur or not? Some say yes

---

* https://www.pwc.com/us/en/industry/entertainment-media/publications/consumer-intelligence-series/assets/pwc-consumer-intellgience-series-future-of-work-june-2016.pdf

because, again, she has invested her own money and runs her own business, while others say no because she does not have enough autonomy. A McDonald's franchisee cannot control price, menu, machine and terminal selection, human resource practices, advertising, branding, or just about anything. Even the location of a franchise is driven by McDonald's more than the franchisee.

So, back to Uber drivers, they have no control over price and have limited control over most of everything else in the transaction. So are they really freelancers, or independent entrepreneurs, or, in fact, perhaps a new form of exploited workers with no benefits and no minimum wage? Well, in an epic court battle between Uber and regulators in the United Kingdom in October, 2016, it was determined that Uber drivers should be treated as employees and not independent freelancers, and thus be entitled to minimum wage, paid vacations, and other benefits of employment. My point with this story is that just because someone is not working as a full-time employee does not, at least in my view, qualify them as entrepreneurs. In this book, I will be focusing on numerous forms of entrepreneurship that have emerged in recent years that allow for more autonomy, albeit as a freelancer, small business owner/operator, or as a startup.

Boyd Cohen, Ph.D.
EADA Business School
& Universitat de Vic

Introduction

"Never before has the world seen so many societies organized around the principles of market competition and capital accumulation, which systematically produce extremes of selfish individualism, inequalities of wealth and crippling assaults on natural ecosystems."

David Bollier
Think Like a Commoner

ENTREPRENEURSHIP IN A POST-CAPITALIST SOCIETY

In the late Andy Grove's book, *Only the Paranoid Survive*, he discussed the mammoth challenges Intel faced throughout its history and the times when they needed to remake the company in order to survive the global competitive landscape. He also discussed the point in time when a company or society is facing an inflection point and must consider radical changes to survive and thrive:

"An event, development or confluence of events and developments over time that result(s) in a significant change in the progress of a company. Industry, sector, economy, or geopolitical situation. An inflection point can be considered a turning point after which a dramatic hange, with either positive or negative results, is expected to result. Most strategic inflection points appear slowly, and are often not clear until events are viewed in retrospect. Denial is often present in the early stages."

I believe we are at such an inflection point. As I highlighted in the preface, things are changing in important ways. Technology is improving lives in many ways, while also replacing jobs at an unprecedented rate. Income inequality is growing not shrinking; the rich are getting richer while even highly educated people struggle to find stable employment and incomes. Calls for some form of a basic income are growing in countries like The Netherlands, Spain, Canada, Namibia, the United Kingdom, and even in Silicon Valley in the United States, as the writing is on the wall that technological unemployment could further deteriorate social conditions for the lower and middle class. These challenges to a stable and prosperous society have drawn calls for challenging our understanding of the market economy, leading to suggestions for a shift to a post-capitalist society.

If we may, in fact, already be in the transition to a post-capitalist society, then what does this mean for entrepreneurs, not just in Silicon Valley, but globally? This book is about understanding the implications of the post-capitalist society for our knowledge about entrepreneurship around the globe and challenges many of our underlying assumptions about how entrepreneurs form startups, with what objectives, and the role, or lack thereof, for startup investors in a post-capitalist society. Furthermore, this book will have a strong focus on exploring real emerging stories and thinking about different forms of post-capitalist entrepreneurship (PCE) with chapters dedicated to subjects such as alternative currencies (local, crypto, and time banking) and the emergence of distributed autonomous organizations (DAOs), leveraging distributed ledger technologies like the blockchain. It will also explore some hybrid approaches which are on a continuum between market capitalism and PCE, such as platform cooperatives within the sharing economy and benefit corporations (e.g., B Corporations).

Below, I have laid out a framework that is guiding my own thinking and research in the area of PCE. It emerges from my last 15 years of experience as a researcher and consultant in innovation, sustainability, technology, urban issues, and, of course, entrepreneurship. In summary, the writing is on the wall that something must change with our current market-based economic model or we will have even more social unrest and potentially catastrophic challenges to the earth's ability to support our swelling global population (estimates suggest we will go beyond 10 billion by 2100 with the overwhelming majority living in crowded cities).

The first column in the table on the following page (Failures of Neoliberal Market-Based Capitalism) suggests major problems on the horizon, however the latter columns (Emergence of Alternative Tools and Policies to Counteract Failures, Next: Entrepreneur and Values/Mindsets) start painting a more optimistic picture of the future in a post-capitalist society. While this introductory chapter focuses mostly on column 1, the rest of the book focuses on constructive framing, tools, and insights from pioneering entrepreneurs, thought leaders, enlightened governments, and even hardcore capitalists like some in the venture capital community, who have started to show clues as to how a transition to post-capitalist entrepreneurship could pave the way toward a more prosperous and egalitarian future.

POST-CAPITALIST ENTREPRENEURSHIP

Failures of neoliberal market-based capitalism	Emergence of alternative tools and policies to counteract failures	Next: Entrepreneur	Values/ mindsets
		Entrepreneurs within traditional market economies	
Decoupling of GDP growth and prosperity and job growth	**Alternative to salaries**		Embeddedness
· Industry 4.0/automation	· On-demand/freelance	Sustainable entrepreneurship	
· Growing income inequality	· Universal basic income		Synchronized
· Global outsourcing	· Local production and consumption	For-benefit entrepreneurs (**Chapter 2**)	
			Social justice
		Civic entrepreneurs (Urban Entrepreneurship)	
Financialization	**Alternative currencies (Chapter 4)**		Commons
· Growing % of GDP going to financial services	· Local paper currencies permit high velocity of local transactions and disincent financialization	P2P exchange networks and platform cooperatives (**Chapter 3**)	
· Growing consumer and national debts	· Digital currencies decrease dependence on state and enable distributed platforms	Peer Production and Consumption networks (**Chapter 1**)	Reframing value creation and exchange
· Venture capital and capital markets out of synch w/social and ecological systems	· Timebanks and other noncash mechanisms for value exchange		
	· Crowdfunding and alt financing	Distributed autonomous organizations (DAOs) (**Chapter 5**)	
Negative environmental externalities	**Alternative economic models**		
· Climate change	· Carbon markets (*Climate Capitalism*)	Commons-based entrepreneurship (**Chapter 1**)	
· Loss of biodiversity	· Sharing economy (*O&E, TFSC, CMR*)		
· Deforestation	· Circular economy (*Marie Curie*)	*Post-capitalist entrepreneurship*	

The layout of the book is as follows:

CHAPTER 1: TOWARD COMMONS-BASED ENTREPRENEURSHIP

The assumption in classical approaches to entrepreneurship is that entrepreneurs need to build a competitive advantage by developing and protecting intellectual property. In a post-capitalist society, protecting intellectual property gives way to an entirely different approach to value creation and extraction. Rather than seeking to protect any expertise, post-capitalist entrepreneurs treat innovation and value creation as an open process, whereby the community (virtual or physical or both) participate in the innovation process and have unlimited access to the tools that are codeveloped by the community. Instead of consumers, users become participants and build on the work of others.

The concept of the commons, whereby community members collaborate in the sharing or coproduction of resources (digital, physical, natural), has gained steam as a way to frame post-capitalist activity. While capitalism encourages scarcity of resources and protected intellectual property, PCE encourages abundance and access. This chapter is dedicated to exploring the commons as a way to frame PCE and will look at some emerging paradigms and tools for enabling commons-based PCE. This leads to big questions for entrepreneurs such as what kind of organization should they form, how can they make enough money to survive or thrive if they "give" their creations to the commons, and more. In this chapter, we will explore answers to these questions and alternatives to intellectual property protection such as General Public License (GPL), Creative Commons, and Open Hardware licensing. I will also explore several examples of commons-based PCE activities such as open-source software, open-source hardware, Fab Labs, and maker spaces.

CHAPTER 2: FOR-BENEFIT STARTUPS

I do not believe that we will immediately, or maybe even in the medium term, observe a disappearance of startups seeking to scale through more traditional capitalist models. However, I believe we will witness a series of transitionary approaches that are some form of hybrid model between profit-seeking enterprises and PCE. For me, the best place to explore transitionary approaches is for-benefit startups that have increasingly found legal standing in the United States and abroad. B Corporations (B corps) are firms that have voluntarily committed to legally bind themselves to meet a high standard of social and environmental performance.

This chapter will be dedicated to exploring the emergence of B Corps (nearly 2,000 around the world and counting), finding what the process of establishing B Corp status entails, and highlighting some exciting examples of entrepreneurs who are embracing legally binding nonmarket objectives into their strategy and operations. I will also explore the challenges B Corps face in finding investors who are willing to accept, or ideally embrace, the extra commitments made by these firms and the likely slower process for obtaining their return on investment. B Corps may not be truly post-capitalist, but they certainly provide insights into a promising transitionary approach to a PCE society.

CHAPTER 3: ALTERNATIVE CURRENCIES AND PLACE-BASED PCE

What is money really? It is merely a mechanism for exchanging value between two or multiple parties. Before the introduction of paper currency backed by national and regional governments (referred to as fiat currency), gold and other metals were used to facilitate exchange. Before gold, there were many other systems like bartering whereby I made something you valued and you paid me with something I valued. We are seeing a resurgence around the globe of a range of alternative currencies from local paper currencies to digital cryptocurrencies, time banking, and gift economies. This chapter is dedicated to exploring entrepreneurship that leverages, creates, or supports alternative currencies.

CHAPTER 4: FROM THE PLATFORM DEATHSTARS TO TECHNOLOGY-ENABLED PLATFORM COOPERATIVISM

We have witnessed a rapid growth in the use of platforms for connecting peers and businesses to each other. While this has been labeled as the sharing economy, many of these enterprises have been accused of exploitative behavior and damaging, rather than improving communities. Airbnb, Uber, Deliveroo, and others have been sued and even banned in countries around the globe for skirting regulation and exploiting "independent contractors" who are really employees without minimum wages, benefits, or health care. This has given the sharing economy and its entrepreneurs a bad name. In fact, some, such as Shareable's Neal Gorenflo, refer to global sharing economy startups as "Platform Deathstars." But, there are thousands of other sharing-economy projects, some technology-enabled and some not, which have embraced more of a commons approach to sharing. In this chapter, I will introduce the sharing business model compass and sharing business model canvas I developed with my colleague Pablo Muñoz after researching dozens of sharing-economy business models and introduce the growth of platform cooperatives as an interesting alternative approach to the creation of sharing-economy enterprises.

CHAPTER 5: THE DISTRIBUTED AUTONOMOUS ORGANIZATION

Beyond platform cooperatives, which still technically operate within capitalist models, there is a new PCE model called a distributed autonomous organization (DAO), which has only emerged in the past few years. A DAO is basically a mashup between open-source software (see Chapter 1) and platform cooperatives (see Chapter 4). A DAO is technically not even an enterprise but rather based on software developed and enhanced through the community. But rather than say Wikipedia, which is an open-source tool for sharing knowledge, DAOs are open-source tools for facilitating exchanges between peers. Think Uber, without Uber in the middle whereby drivers would gain 100% of the transaction value. This is not science fiction either. Backed primarily by distributed ledgers like the blockchain which was initially conceived to support Bitcoin (Chapter 3), DAOs are emerging as we speak or as I write. Can DAO's operate globally, leveraging distributed global tech to support local ecosystems and P2P interaction? How will conflicts be resolved? Is it really possible to have a P2P platform with no intermediary? Will there be any revenue model that emerges for the collaborative group that develops and maintains the DAO platform? In this chapter, I seek to answer, or at least shed light on, some of these questions while providing some insights on emerging experiments of DAOs.

CHAPTER 6: VENTURE CAPITAL IS DEAD IN A PCE WORLD

Winner-take-all capitalism will remain a driver in the United States but is increasingly at odds with the 99% movement. When entrepreneurs are no longer driven to own the world, the venture capital model no longer applies. How will startups be financed in a PCE world? In this chapter, I will explore numerous alternatives to venture capital for financing startups with a strong focus on a range of crowdfunding platforms and for just embracing fully lean startup methodologies for PCE. I will also discuss the growing slow money movement and the increasing number of impact investors who seek to invest in enterprises with a strong social and environmental mandate. Also, I will discuss ways in which civic entrepreneurs are funding their projects through procurement for innovation programs from local and regional governments.

CHAPTER 7: BACK TO THE FUTURE

Throughout the book, I have explored a wide range of alternative forms of organizing in a post-capitalist economy. While each chapter has been treated as a focus on discrete topics, frequently with little attention to the territory of post-capitalist entrepreneurs, in this chapter, I will turn my attention to what could happen if a specific territory, or cities in particular, could embrace all of the forms of PCE discussed in this book, along with other post-capitalist topics such as universal basic income and Fab cities, to go back to the future, merging concepts from bygone eras along with emerging technologies such as blockchain and 3D printing to remake our economies from the ground up.

As you can see, this book is ambitious and also fairly broad in focus as I hope to cover the main themes relevant to entrepreneurship in a post-capitalist society, which is a complex and rapidly evolving phenomenon. While of course I would be thrilled if you would want to read the whole book from cover to cover, I suspect many of you will not; hopefully, this chapter summary will help you decide the chapters you are most interested in.

If you want to continue the dialog on social media, I will be using the hashtag #PostCapEnt to track and participate in an ongoing conversation with the global community. Happy reading!

1

Commons Entrepreneurship

In 2003, frustrated with the lack of access to broadband infrastructure in rural Catalunya (Gurb) near the Pyrenees, Ramon Roca decided to take matters into his own hands. There he discovered that he could use WiFi to connect to a public building in a nearby town called Vic (as a side note, I am a joint professor at the Universitat de Vic). At the time, Ramon was an IT professional with Oracle, so he had a better idea than most about how to pull this off. Early on, however, Ramon felt that there must be thousands of people, at least, living in the rural areas of Catalunya who could benefit from his makeshift model for turning slow WiFi into a broadband connection. Ramon and other community members began requesting access to church steeples and other high points in and around Gurb to place networking equipment in order to facilitate better access to broadband for community members. Thus was born Guifi.net, one of the largest community-based mesh networks in the world. In 2008, Guifi.net had 5,500 working nodes, and by 2013, it had 22,000, and at the time of writing there were more than 32,000 active nodes were active on the network.

What makes Guifi.net unique is that it was never developed to be a revenue-generating initiative. Instead, Roca and early members were committed to the idea that access to high-speed Internet is increasingly a necessity in today's globally connected world and that it is not fair that people choosing to live in rural communities have inadequate access to this fundamental resource because it is not profitable for the private sector to deliver broadband to less densely populated communities. Guifi.net has grown, thanks to sponsors and donations from individuals and corporations over the years. Sure, there is no business model directly associated with Guifi.net. But, it is certain that many entrepreneurs living in remote Catalunya and now in the Valencia region of Spain as well have benefitted from free high-speed access made possible by Guifi.net. Roca's Guifi.net is an example of a growing number of initiatives that can be classified as contributing to the commons.

This chapter is dedicated to exploring the emerging approaches entrepreneurs and communities are taking toward protecting or creating commons which are neither private nor government initiatives. While the concept of the commons has existed for centuries, or perhaps since the beginning of mankind (or even earlier since some argue that animal species have operated with natural commons since before we arrived on the planet), it will still be a new term to many people. Essentially, the commons are resources that are shared with express or unwritten rules for ensuring the survival and growth of physical, digital, or cultural spaces.

In his book, *Think like a Commoner*, David Bollier, global commons expert, defined the commons as (p. 175):

- A social system for the long-term stewardship of resources that preserves shared values and community identity.
- A self-organized system by which communities manage resources (both depletable and replenishable) with minimal or no reliance on the Market or State.
- The wealth that we inherit or create together and must pass on, undiminished or enhanced, to our children. Our collective wealth includes the gifts of nature, civic infrastructure, cultural works, and traditions of knowledge.
- A sector of the economy (and life!) that generates value in ways that are often taken for granted and often jeopardized by the market state.

Drawing from the research of one of the pioneering scholars in the commons' field, Elinor Ostrom, Bollier concludes that in order for something to qualify as a commons, it must involve a community (virtual and/or physical) committed to establishing "boundaries, rules, social norms and sanctions against free riders."[1]

In his book, *Capitalism 3.0*, Peter Barnes suggests that there are three types of commons: nature, community, and culture. Similarly, Michel Bauwens, the founder of the P2P Foundation, identified three forms of commons as well: inherited commons (nature), immaterial commons (culture, knowledge, Internet-enabled/digital), and material commons (co-created products for widespread use and sharing). For a more detailed comparison of market versus commons thinking, please refer to the table in the Appendix.

THE CITY AS A COMMONS

Jane Jacobs, one of the most renowned urbanists of all time, once famously said: *Cities have the capability of providing something for everybody, only because, and only when, they are created by everybody.*[2]

It is impossible to discuss post-capitalist entrepreneurship (PCE) without discussing territory. As my colleague, Pablo Muñoz, and I have discovered through our interviews with urban and civic entrepreneurs, the sense of place that some entrepreneurs feel can have a big influence on the type of entrepreneurial activity they engage in. Cities and neighborhoods are often able to inspire entrepreneurial action oriented toward improving the quality of life for local residents.

In recent years, there has been a growing critique of the perceived privatization of cities through selling of city land to private developers, the growing use of public–private partnership models for managing infrastructure and services frequently thought to be a common good (water, energy, roads, energy, etc.), and the growth of the smart cities movement. The cities as a commons movement has emerged in recent years as an alternative model of governance of cities, whereby citizen quality of life and inclusive access are prioritized over private sector interests.

> The city is a commons in the sense that it is a shared resource that belongs to all of its inhabitants. As such, the commons claim is importantly aligned with the idea behind the "right to the city"—the right to be part of the creation of the city, the right to be part of the decisionmaking processes shaping the lives of city inhabitants, and the power of inhabitants to shape decisions about the collective resource in which we all have a stake.[3]

As my colleagues Duncan McClaren and Julian Agyeman discuss in detail in *Sharing Cities*, much of the emerging sharing economy has direct implications for the city as a commons where we are witnessing a range of sharing activity which either is oriented toward cultivating commons (e.g., Repair Café and bikesharing services) or seem to be new ways of privatizing and monetizing resources and people in urban areas (e.g., Airbnb, Task Rabbit, and Uber). While many of the projects highlighted in this book are not necessarily bound by territory, particularly those leveraging digital platforms for distributed governance, consumption, and production, many others have a decidedly local flavor to them. Below, I will highlight just two growing trends in urban commoning, community land trusts and farmers' markets. However, the last chapter of this book is dedicated to exploring how a range of post-capitalist models could combine and happen at an urban scale.

Community Land Trusts

In Boston, people in the Dudley Street neighborhood formed one (Community Land Trust) in 1988 to buy vacant land and determine how it could best serve the community. Today there are six hundred new and rehabbed homes—all with a cap on resale prices—plus gardens, a common area, parks, and playgrounds. These efforts revitalized the neighborhood without displacing local residents, as would have happened through private property and gentrification.[4]

What Barnes didn't directly mention in his summary is the potential for such efforts to be generative or supportive of local economic conditions. For example, smart choices by the neighborhood could result in improved property prices in the long term, like by choosing to add public parks instead of more buildings. Or, protect and encourage local retailers instead of selling the property to the largest bidder who could be a big box store.

As has been documented frequently in recent years, several high-profile cities such as San Francisco, London, New York, and Vancouver are gentrifying so rapidly that they are becoming unaffordable to the masses. Community land trusts (CLTs) are gaining interest as an alternative, commons-based model to ensuring affordable housing in an otherwise out-of-reach housing market.

Recently in London, such a CLT was created together with market housing in a partnership with a traditional housing developer, the East London Community Land Trust, and an affordable housing activist group, Citizens UK. The collaboration emerged after the developer, Galliford Try, purchased the St. Clement's Hospital, whose doors had been shuttered a decade earlier. The CLT used a combination of public and private funds to lease a portion of the land that Galliford Try had acquired. While Galliford Try is developing the majority of the site for luxury condos, this collaboration led to the creation of permanently affordable housing in the same development. At the time of this writing, 23 CLT units were being occupied by qualifying tennants. The CLT units are priced, not at market rates, but rather at a price tied to local median wages. The land is leased by the CLT, but the units are purchased by local members of the CLT. When owners of a CLT wishes to sell their unit in the future, they are bound to sell at a predetermined formula tied to the median income at the time of sale, thus assuring in perpetuity some level of affordability for those units.

Farmers' Markets

Farmers' markets and artisanal fairs are types of commercial commons that are growing in communities around the globe. In the United States, there are more than 8,000 active farmers' markets, up from just a few hundred in the 1990s.[5] While many farmers' markets are temporary, open, for example, on weekends during peak growing seasons, others are more permanent locations for local producers and consumers to transact in a physical space, without involving the intermediary grocery store. In Barcelona, where I live, we are lucky to have such dedicated physical markets in nearly every neighborhood of the city. La Boqueria, in the famed Las Ramblas, gets all the attention from tourists, but residents can get locally produced fruits, vegetables, and meats frequently within walking distance of their homes.

A recent study in the United Kingdom identified 25 benefits to local communities and the local economy from hosting vibrant farmers' markets. These benefits included 3.5 billion pounds in farmers' market revenues throughout the United Kingdom with a three times multiplier from direct and indirect impacts, a 25% increase in foot traffic in town centers hosting farmers' markets, and the creation of high numbers of employment (105,000 in the United Kingdom) and food businesses and startups (47,000 in the United Kingdom).[6] Also, farmers' markets offer the opportunity for aspiring food entrepreneurs to test their concepts, to meet prospective customers face to face, and to validate the potential of the opportunity in ways that go beyond the traditional food supply system.

Merging the concept of food markets with technology platforms allows the emergence of modern models for connecting local food producers with food consumers. For many years, I had the pleasure of living in British Columbia, first in Victoria, then in Vancouver. In Victoria, I had the opportunity to meet the founder of Small Potatoes Urban Delivery (SPUD), David Van Seters, who had previously been a management consultant with KPMG before he turned his attention to the unsustainable and unequal practices in the farming business. Recognizing the distance the average food basket travels to get to someone's home in British Columbia, combined with the fertilizers and pesticides used in much of the agricultural industry and the small margins afforded to local farmers, Van Seters founded SPUD to change the model and disintermediate the sector. SPUD would go to local farmers and commit to buying 100% of their produce if they agreed to transition to organic production. While SPUD was encouraging the transformation of local agriculture to organic, they were simultaneously building a direct channel to local consumers interested in quality local food and the convenience of having the food delivered to their home. To reduce the ecological footprint of delivery, SPUD developed a logistics model where they would deliver to certain neighborhoods on specific days of the week. Van Seters had achieved his transformational goals of the local food industry and sold most of his stake in 2010, after reaching $18 million (Canadian) in annual sales. Later in this chapter, I will introduce an example of an entrepreneur blending the maker movement with the local food movement.

COMMONS-BASED PEER PRODUCTION

In the *Wealth of Networks*, Yochai Benkler introduced the concept of commons-based peer production (CBPP). As Michel Bauwens suggested in a recent article in Evonomics,[7] CBPP is a new pathway of value creation and distribution, where peer-to-peer infrastructure allows individuals to communicate, self-organize, and, ultimately, to cocreate nonrivalrous use value, in the form of digital commons of knowledge, software, and design.

While Benkler and Bauwens frame CBPP primarily as a digital commons model, I believe there are also examples of CBPP that either emerge exclusively in the physical world or at the growing blend between the physical and digital worlds, such as with open 3D printing models which I will discuss later.

Open Software

The concept of open software, as opposed to proprietary closed software, is a natural starting point for thinking about the commons and new forms of PCE. Any discussion of open software usually begins with references to Linux, one of the first, and the most ubiquitous open software projects in the world. In 1991, Linus Torvalds, a 21-year-old university student in Finland, frustrated with the cost of the Unix mainframe operating system, had the audacity to attempt to develop his own operating system. But instead of treating this project as a closed, market-based software development, Linus decided to publish the early code in an online forum. Within a few years, this personal project of Linus had created an open software movement around the globe.

While the Linux software platform is based on the principles of CBPP and open access to all, that does not mean it has not created economically viable entrepreneurial opportunities. By 2011, researchers valued the ecosystem of startups and companies that had built businesses leveraging Linux at $49 billion (USD)[8] and in 2015, the Linux Foundation published a report estimating the value of the Linux code to represent the equivalent of $5 billion of programming costs had Linux been built as a private operating system with paid programmers.[9]

Crunchbase, a leading website for information about funding for startups, currently lists 170 startups in their Linux category. Red Hat may be one of the most famous and successful former startups leveraging Linux. Red Hat was founded in 1995, just 4 years after Linus started the opensource movement, with a goal of developing open-source software leveraging Linux for sale to corporations (enterprise software). In 2012, Red Hat became the first open-source company to hit $1 billion (USD) in revenue. With 10,000 employees and revenues of $2 billion (USD) per year, and a market value of $13.2 billion (USD), Red Hat is far from a prototypical post-capitalist enterprise. Yet, their continued commitment to the open source movement demonstrates that it is possible to be financially successful while contributing to the commons through open-source software.

While many readers are probably clear on this, I suspect many others are reading this and wondering, how can companies committed to developing open-source software generate that kind of revenue, or perhaps any revenue at all? It is important to note that building tools leveraging open source software does not mean you have to commit to giving it away for free. There are business models where open-source software companies charge customers for using the software but also allow their customers or the broader community to improve the code. In the past year, I had the chance to communicate several times with the founder of ShareTribe, Juho Makkonen. Sharetribe is a Finnish software as a service (SaaS) company that allows sharing-economy startups to quickly launch a customized sharing platform. While ShareTribe is built on open source code, they charge a subscription fee for their customers that varies depending on the size of the customer's user base. If at any point a customer wishes to further customize their sharing platform beyond the current code base offered through the SaaS model, they can obtain the current code base for free from ShareTribe, but then ShareTribe no longer supports or hosts the software.

In the case of Red Hat, much of their revenue comes from selling unlimited service and support to their enterprise customers, usually via monthly or annual subscriptions. Given its size, it is not surprising that Red Hat has diversified its product offerings and revenues over time. Currently, Red Hat is actively pursuing the enterprise cloud infrastructure.[10]

OPEN STANDARDS

Embracing commons thinking, post-capitalist entrepreneurs have participated in the creation and support of a growing number of open standards designed to facilitate information sharing of creative projects. Instead of protecting intellectual property, post-capitalist entrepreneurs embrace the wisdom of the crowd and contribute to the community by sharing their creations. In return, post-capitalist entrepreneurs not only generate good will for their projects but also embrace the community in improving their products and services as well. Here, I will briefly summarize some of the most important standards being applied by these new forms of post-capitalist entrepreneurs.

Creative Commons

Creative Commons (CC) licenses are among the most widely used open standards. CC licenses generally have four potential elements although they can use any combination of them, or selectively leverage some elements: attribution, share alike, noncommercial, and no derivative works. With *attribution*, the user of a CC-licensed design must give credit to (i.e., attribute) their work to the original author of the design. A CC license may allow for future designers to modify the original if it is identified as a *share alike* license. *Noncommercial* asserts that users of the originally CC-licensed design are not allowed to reuse or alter the design for commercial purposes. Finally, *no derivative* allows for the replication and distribution of the CC-licensed design but does not allow for modifications to the original design such as the share alike option. Thingverse, a community for sharing information and designs of 3D objects, states their preference for 3D designers who are willing to publish their designs under CC licensing.

General Public License

General Public Licenses (GPLs) are among the most liberal open standards available to developers and are commonly used with open software and documents. For the most part, a GPL allows others to copy, distribute, or modify the software or document, usually for free, without much restriction, if any. While this sounds like a dumb idea if you want to actually find a way to somehow make a living off of your hard work, it is important to note that not all commons entrepreneurs aspire to profit from their innovation, instead many are keen to have their creations in use in the world, as well as have others add to their work to improve its utility. In some cases, such as Ramon Roca mentioned in the introduction to this chapter, the originator of a commons product may still benefit without generating revenue directly from building a commons solution. For example, Roca can now travel freely throughout much of Catalunya and Valencia and be assured of access to high-speed bandwidth through the growth of Guifi.net.* Furthermore, there are still several ways to generate income off of your own creations without necessarily selling your original source code. At the end of this chapter, I list several such ways in which commons entrepreneurs are generating income while still committing to nourishing the commons.

Massachusetts Institute of Technology (MIT)

The MIT license beats out even GPL as far as flexibility for followers is concerned. MIT licenses allow followers to replicate, modify, and even sell the design or software without restriction, except that the licensing agreement must be incorporated into its future use. The MIT license is generally included as follows:

Permission is hereby granted, free of charge, to any person obtaining a copy of this software and associated documentation files (the "Software"), to deal in the Software without restriction, including without limitation

---

* Guifi.net has its own commons license, XOLN, which focuses on net neutrality, and open and free Internet applications.

the rights to use, copy, modify, merge, publish, distribute, sublicense, and/ or sell copies of the Software, and to permit persons to whom the Software is furnished to do so, subject to the following conditions:

The above copyright notice and this permission notice shall be included in all copies or substantial portions of the Software.

Open Access (Education)

It is not a coincidence that I place open educational resources after MIT, which has been a leading academic institution in so many areas of the open movement, including the MIT license mentioned above, the Fab Lab Foundation discussed later, and open educational resources such as curriculum, courses, and online videos. Ironically, MIT is also unfortunately the same academic institution that decided to prosecute Aaron Schwartz, the brilliant programmer and former executive of Reddit who believed that academic research, much of which is financed by state and federal governments, should be freely available to all. In pursuit of this quest, Schwartz decided to download and share millions of academic articles he acquired from an MIT server. This is not the place to provide more history here as I do not have the space for it (there is actually a movie or two about his plight), but unfortunately Schwartz killed himself rather than go to prison for this "crime."

Yet, the argument that academic research should be made publicly available to all has received significant attention from the scholarly community. In his book, *Think Like a Commoner*, Bollier laments the eroding of the commons, particularly through the growing collaborations between the state and the private sector in targeted research projects, resulting in profitable patents for the private sector even when the original innovation was funded partially or wholly from taxpayer dollars. The open-access movement has gained steam with several journals committing to some form of open licensing such as CC, while the Open CourseWare Consortium promotes standards for opening up academic and course content to the world to make the acquisition of knowledge accessible to those who cannot afford or do not have the time to attend universities. Meanwhile, many of the most important academic journals across all disciplines remain behind a paywall. Perhaps inspired by Schwarz, Sci-Hub emerged recently as a web platform for obtaining academic articles from such journals. Sci-Hub proudly notes on their homepage that it is "the first pirate website in the world to provide mass and public access to tens of millions of research papers,"[11] and that it currently contains 58 million "and growing" academic articles for free to anyone with a browser.

This commitment to open-access education has not been lost on entrepreneurs who have entered the space with a range of tools and platforms to facilitate access to open content. Coursera, founded by Daphne Koller and Andrew Yanta in 2012, offers more than 1,000 courses via their platform to more than 20 million subscribed users. While Coursera is not a PCE, but rather a traditional for-profit, venture-capital-backed startup having raised more than nearly US$150 million, Coursera's model does work to democratize access to education to a broader audience than those who can afford and gain access to degree programs from the 140 participating universities, including Stanford, University of Michigan, Duke, the Technical University of Munich, and my alma mater, University of Colorado, who offer access to their courses to Coursera members who pay US$73 a month for unlimited course offerings.

Meanwhile, edX more closely reflects the PCE values discussed throughout this book. Founded by MIT and Harvard, also in 2012, edX is committed to offering free access to massive online open courses (MOOC) and have also embraced open software, Open edX, to allow other educators free access to the open software driving edX. As of early 2017, edX was offering 1,380 courses from 90 partner institutions in 30 different subject areas from business to physics, law, and medicine.

Open Hardware

While open software had a major head start, in recent years, designers of hardware have increasingly embraced the commons mentality and are finding hybrid models that connect their physical designs to software that allow them to share, and modify and improve their designs. Consider the story of the Global Village Construction Set (GVCS). First introduced at the University of Missouri in 2008, GVCS aims to design 50 different farm machines in a modular format and publish the designs leveraging open hardware principles. GVCS is really a social movement founded on the principles of self-efficiency. They believe that everyone has the right to provide for themselves, and by opening the designs for free use by anyone, they are empowering anyone with access to land and basic fabrication equipment to be able to farm for personal consumption and/or commercial purposes. The GVCS community has estimated that their machines are eight times cheaper to produce than those available from farm equipment manufacturers. Like other forms of open-source licensing discussed above, the GVCS community even encourages what they refer to as "distributive economics," empowering entrepreneurs around the globe with access to fabrication equipment to download the designs and produce them for sale to local farmers.

The growing interest in embracing the commons from product designers led to the creation of the Open Hardware and Design Alliance. One of the fastest growing areas of the open hardware movement is in the exploding 3D printing sector. Several platforms have emerged that facilitate makers who are using 3D printers to share their designs with others, for free or for a fee. Thingverse, Pinshipe, and Open3model Viewer are just a few of them. Thingverse, for example, considers itself to be a "thriving design community for discovering, making, and sharing 3D printable things. As the world's largest 3D printing community, we believe that everyone should be encouraged to create and remix 3D things, no matter their technical expertise or previous experience. In the spirit of maintaining an open platform, all designs are encouraged to be licensed under a CC license, meaning that anyone can use or alter any design."[12] The Fab Lab Network and Foundation, founded by MIT, represents a further evolution of the open hardware and the 3D printing sector by not only facilitating access to open hardware designs but also enabling access to 3D printing and other tools of the maker movement to communities around the globe.

FAB LABS AND MAKER SPACES

The maker movement shares the following three characteristics which capture its transformative potential[13]: (1) Makers create digital designs and prototype them with the help of digital fabrication tools. (2) A guiding principle is that makers share these designs and collaborate in online communities. (3) Makers use common design file standards, that is, the designs are, in principle, compatible with commercial manufacturers systems.

Fab Labs represent a growing movement, started by MIT, for more advanced, accessible, and shared makerspaces. For a makerspace to be considered for membership into the Fab Lab Network, it must meet several requirements regarding openness and accessibility to the local community, technology tools available (including 3D printers, laser cutters, milling machines, and much more), and a commitment to sharing learning locally and with the Fab Lab Network around the globe:

The Fab Lab Network is an open, creative community of fabricators, artists, scientists, engineers, educators, students, amateurs, and professionals, aged 5 to 75 years, with more than 1,100 Fab Labs located in more than 40 countries. From community-based labs to advanced research centers, Fab Labs share the goal of democratizing access to the tools for technical invention. This community is simultaneously a manufacturing network, a distributed technical education campus, and a distributed research laboratory working to digitize fabrication, inventing the next generation of manufacturing and personal fabrication.

Stories abound around the globe of how commons-based entrepreneurs are leveraging local Fab Labs for reinventing how we make products, simultaneously challenging how our economy could become more inclusive and sustainable. Take Eugenia Morpurgo, an Italian designer and graduate of the Eindhoven Design Academy, who created a new type of company leveraging the Fab Lab in Gent for her inspiration. AnOtherShoe seeks to become:

> A new model for shoe production based on shared knowledge and local manufacturing, through small scale and on demand digital fabrication. A lasercutter is used to create all the components of the shoes.

As a committed PCE, Morpurgo's AnOtherShoe enables download it yourself (DIY), make it yourself (MIY), assemble it yourself (AIY), and of course, wear it yourself (WIY), with all of the resources freely available from the website, anothershoe.net. Also, Morpurgo's commitment to environmental responsibility is evident in the design of the shoe which allows for easy disassembly in order to repair, instead of discard, shoes that break down over time.

From Extractive to Generative

Having a PhD in business and having spent the past 15 plus years teaching MBA students how to build successful startups, I have frequently been guilty of encouraging students and other entrepreneurial teams how to create walls around their proprietary technology and resources. Yet, in recent years, I have come to recognize this to be a 20th century model leftover from the industrial revolution. The old model focuses on extracting value of natural and human resources while trying to protect intellectual property. The new model, more appropriate in the digital age, is to explore how entrepreneurial action can be open and generative as opposed to exploitative. Generative entrepreneurship seeks to enrich the community of users and other stakeholders as much or more than the founders, and is at the core of what I consider to be post-capitalist entrepreneurship.

Crowdfunding platforms have been revolutionary around the globe as they have allowed entrepreneurs, artists, and makers to fund their projects without having to prove their potential worth to (or sell equity to) traditional startup investors. In this sense, all crowdfunding platforms have been generative, helping entrepreneurs around the world achieve their dreams.

Goteo was founded in 2011 in Spain by Enric Senabre and Oliver Schulbaum, whom I have had the pleasure to meet with several times since moving to Barcelona in 2015. Goteo.org is a crowdfunding platform supporting projects "which, apart from giving individual rewards, also generate a collective return through fomenting the commons, open code and/ or free knowledge."[14] Goteo itself, like several of the organizations already highlighted in this chapter, are fully committed to the open-source movement, publishing their code and actively supporting others to replicate Goteo in other parts of the world.

Goteo is a nonprofit foundation, yet it does have a revenue model, receiving a 4% commission on all successfully funded projects on the platform. In 2016, Goteo raised 1,172,607 euros, successfully funding 77% of proposed projects with an average donation of 48.5 euros. Unlike the Red Hat founders and management team, however, the Goteo founders do not expect to become millionaires, generating a modest 160,000 euros since founding Goteo. Goteo is clearly a crowdfunding platform that is committed to supporting the commons as a generative model. In Chapter 6, I will go into more detail of Goteo's crowdfunding model and provide some examples of PCEs leveraging the platform.

What Is the "Business Model" for a Commons Entrepreneur?

Sure this book is about a new type of entrepreneur, one who is less focused on extractive approaches and more interested in creating real value for users and society. In this chapter, I have introduced the growing interest in contributing to the commons through a CBPP model for digital, physical, or hybrid solutions. But, having been an entrepreneur several times myself, and a business school professor and consultant for close to two decades,

I do not suggest that entrepreneurial behavior should go unrewarded from an economic perspective. So, if a commons entrepreneur is focused on growing the commons, how in the world can he or she make a living with his or her project? While I will talk about basic income in the last chapter as a possible scenario for creating an income floor for PCEs who make little or no income from their projects, it is also important to consider alternative revenue and business models that show promise for CBPP models.

In January of 2017, I had the pleasure of meeting with Guillaume Teyssie, a 29-year-old French engineer who previously worked in the smart cities space. Along with his partner, Loic Le Goueff, a 27-year-old Swiss national agrarian, they launched a startup called Aquapioneers. Through access to Barcelona's Green Fab Lab, the pair had managed to design and build a closed loop aquaponics device which can be used by homeowners and renters to produce their own vegetables at their homes with minimum investment and low operating costs. While aquaponics is not a new solution, and there are many companies pursuing traditional venture-capital-backed models, such as Brighter Farms, what makes Aquapioneers so interesting is that they have committed to the maker community and to open source hardware. In fact, they are making their design freely available for downloading and printing at the more than 1,100 Fab Labs around the world.

You may ask, well how do they make money if they give away their designs for free? Welcome to the world of PCE. Guillaume and his cofounder were trying to figure out this same question, which is why he sought me for mentoring the project. Aquapioneers was one of 15 participants in Barcelona's peer-to-peer incubator, La Comunificadora. There is no single answer to how a project like Aquapioneers could allow the founders to dedicate themselves full time to this project while making a decent living. Yet, there are several emerging approaches to consider. I will highlight several options we discussed leveraging other commons-based projects around the globe.

1. *Rely on the Crowd* I have already discussed crowdfunding and, in particular, Goteo as an interesting tool for supporting generativity as opposed to extractive behavior. Some PCEs have done very well by relying on the crowd to support their initiatives through a range of offerings. As Goteo suggests, funders of projects on their platform may choose to donate to the project because it is aligned with their values and they empathize with the project's founders, and they in turn may receive prioritized access to the files (e.g., in the case of Aquapioneers, they could allow

early contributors to a crowdfunding campaign, priority or specialized access to the design files, or discounted services or products). For example, Aquapioneers is considering launching a crowdfunding campaign where one of the options is to have Aquapioneers 3D print the funder's aquapionics device. Of course, this model only works well when the funder is geographically close to the founders. On that topic, I suggested offering a higher priced option in a crowdfunding campaign where one of the founders would also go to the funder's home to help set it up and meet the family, etc. This could create more community for the PCE while generating some extra revenue for the founders.

2. *Open Source but Offer a SaaS Model* There are also models like Share Tribe which rely on open source principles, but there is still value for the user to pay for a SaaS solution. For example, what if they could find other Fab Labs around the world interested in offering similar models in their own communities? Aquapioneers could focus on continually upgrading and diversifying their portfolio of aquaponics 3D products, and give priority access to the design files to Fab Labs around the world, in return for a monthly service fee.

3. *Join the Emerging Fab Market* The Fab Market, a project from Fab Lab Barcelona, is creating a market place for open-source 3D designs. In the words of Cat Johnson from Sharable.net, the Fab Market:

> curates, tests, and offers products from makers and designers around the world. The group exists at the intersection of the maker movement and the open-source movement .... People purchase open-source designs of products they want, and then head to one of the nearly 1,000 Fab Labs in the global Fab Lab Network, where they're created using computer numeric control machines, laser cutters, 3D Printers and other tools.

4. *Create Some Form of Franchise Model for Different Sectors* Referring back to Guillaume's challenge, we discussed different subsectors of potential users, private and commercial, who could be interested in their model. Yet, at the time of our conversation, their team consisted of the two founders and no one else. They would have significant challenges going after different segments themselves. But what if they identified different segments, and geographies, and empowered other commons-oriented entrepreneurs to create their own enterprises (like franchise models)? For example, the education sector could be very interested in their aquaponics models as a growing

number of school districts around the globe are embracing STEM, STEAM, or even ESTEAM education. While I won't go into details around these different educational models, STEM represents Science, Technology, Engineering, and Math, while STEAM adds arts to the equation and ESTEAM adds Entrepreneurship as well. (For a longer discussion of these models, see my last book, *The Emergence of the Urban Entrepreneur.*) Other sectors for aquaponics could be organic restaurants, grocery stores, or the direct to home model. Aquaponics could offer a service support system for a monthly fee to entrepreneurs around the globe interested in embracing these sectors. Service could include everything from direct seminars or videos on how to make and sell the aquaponics devises, how to support users, etc. And, in the spirit of the open-source community, some of these empowered entrepreneurs could also enrich Aquapioneers offering by improving the designs. For example, the Aquapioneers team tested their designs at a Fab Lab in Uruguay. Within 5 days, a local fabrication team had improved the LED lighting designs.

5. *Consulting and Teaching* As commons entrepreneurs develop deep expertise in their chosen fields, they could leverage that vast knowledge to offer advice to a range of actors who may be interested in learning from them. This could be from some of the same sectors they are targeting with their products or services. In the case of Aquapioneers, this could be educators (elementary, high school, school districts, and higher education) to assist them in developing their own training programs for students, or aspiring urban farmers interested in embracing aquaponics, or restaurants, etc. Relatedly, this could be turned into some form of MOOC or localized courses.

While it is difficult to anticipate every type of potential revenue stream any type of CBPP entrepreneur may seek, hopefully this list can stimulate thinking in alternative approaches to make a living while also contributing to the commons.

CONCLUSION

I chose to begin this book with a chapter dedicated to entrepreneurship and the commons because I believe there is an underpinning of commons orientation in virtually all forms of post-capitalist enterprising. Yet, the next chapter, dedicated to purpose-driven entrepreneurship, takes a step back from a commitment to post-capitalism, by focusing on firms that are truly committed to purpose, but usually within the market system. Many of these firms are committing to becoming part of the B Corp movement which legally binds firms to focus on ecological and social concerns as well as their bottom line. In fact, SPUD, referenced above in the conversation regarding virtual farmers' markets, is in fact a certified B Corp.

REFERENCES

1. David Bollier, *Think Like a Commoner*, New Society, Gabriola Island, 2014, p. 24.
2. Jane Jacobs, *The Death and Life of Great American Cities*, Random House, New York, 1961.
3. Sheila Foster and Christian Iaione, The city as a commons, *Yale Law & Policy Review*, vol. 281, p. 288, 2016.
4. Peter Barnes, *Capitalism 3.0*, Mcgraw Hill, UK, 2006, p. 136.
5. Randy Bell, Michigan State University, East Lansing August 2013, http://msue.anr.msu.edu/news/public_markets_differ_from_farmers_markets
6. Alan Hallsworth, Nikos Ntounis, Cathy Parker and Simon Quin. *Markets Matter: Reviewing the Evidence & Detecting the Market Effect*, Institute of Place Management, Manchester Metropolitan University, Manchester, UK, 2015.
7. *Solving the Crisis of Extractive Capitalism—Evonomics* 1/15/17, 12(53 PM) http://evonomics.com/post-capitalism-rewards-productive-michel-bauwens/ (accessed March 12, 2017)
8. Sean Michael Kerner, IDC: Linux-Related Spending Could Top $49B by 2011, Internet News, April 2008, http://www.internetnews.com/software/article.php/3739491
9. Estimating the Total Development Cost of Linux Foundation's Collaborative Projects, Linux.com, https://www.linux.com/publications/est mating-totaldevelopment-cost-linux-foundations-collaborative projects (accessed March 4, 2017).
10. Steven Vaughan-Nichols, Red Hat CEO announces a Shift from Client Server to Cloud Computing, ZDNet, http://www.zdnet.com/article/red-hat ceo-announcesa-shift-from-client-server-to-cloud computing (accessed November 2016).
11. Sci-Hub, About http://sci-hub.io (accessed on March 21, 2017).
12. Open Source Ecology Wiki http://opensourceecology.org/wiki/ Global_Village_Construction_Set (accessed February 2017).
13. Chris Anderson, *Makers: The New Industrial Revolution*, Crown Business, New York, 2012.
14. GOTEO FAQ, https://en.goteo.org/faq (accessed March 2017).

2

Benefit Corporations and Associations

The Purpose Economy is defined by the quest for people to have more purpose in their lives. It is an economy where values lies in establishing purpose for employees and customers-through serving needs greater than their own, enabling personal growth, and building community.

Aaron Hurst
The Purpose Economy

Hurst goes on to identify three core elements of purpose, namely personal purpose, social purpose, and societal purpose, and argues that only firms truly committed to purpose will succeed going forward because they are the only ones capable of retaining employees and customers. While Hurst frames this purpose economy within traditional market economies, I am less convinced that firms operating in the market economy will continue to attract and retain employees and customers as the profit motive is often too strong for many of these firms. It is easy for firms to cut corners, like, for example, engage in mass layoffs, when faced with economic difficulties. We see this even sometimes with companies who remain highly profitable. When banks too big to fail (many of whom have great, glossy corporate social responsibility reports) got bailed out by the US government, many continued to engage in significant layoffs even as profits returned in 2011.

Similarly, British Petroleum (BP) years ago sought to rebrand itself as Beyond Petroleum to demonstrate its commitment to environmental sustainability and, in particular, renewable energy. Yet, in hopes of keeping costs down on their new offshore oil well, reportedly saved a few hundred thousand dollars by refusing to conduct some standard tests, resulting in the massive 2010 disaster of the Deepwater Horizon, leading to the loss of 11 lives; an estimated $62 billion in pretax losses[1]; and in the death of 5,000 marine mammals, thousands of sea turtles, 1 million sea birds; and in the contamination of 1,000 miles of coastline.[2] Sound like something a purpose-driven company would do? Yet, if you read their 2009 CSR report (before the accident), their values include responsibility defined as being *committed to the safety and development of our people and the communities in which we operate. We aim for no accidents, no harm to people and no damage to the environment.*

I suggest that a stated commitment to purpose, as suggested by Aaron Hurst, is not enough. Even if some or many leaders of firms reporting a commitment to purpose actually are driven by motives beyond profits, it is often too easy for startups and companies to resort to less sustainable practices when faced with difficult decisions. Yet, there is a subset of the Purpose Economy, if you will, which I believe is worthy of discussion in a book focused on post-capitalist entrepreneurship. Benefit Corporations and B Corps are good examples of new approaches to incorporating businesses, still within the traditional market economy, with purpose embedded into their founding principles.

BENEFIT CORPORATIONS AND CERTIFIED B CORPS

In 2010, I was invited to help implement a type of startup incubator (SB Innovation Open) for the annual Sustainable Brands conference in Monterrey, California. I had the opportunity to interact with Jay Coen Gilbert who was there to discuss a sustainability-oriented certification he and his cofounders had created. The B Lab Foundation had spent the prior few years, developing and launching an early version of the B Corp certification and he was at Sustainable Brands to build traction for it among small and large sustainability-driven enterprises. I found Jay to be articulate and insightful regarding the sustainability challenges we face, and why businesses need to demonstrate more commitment to being part of the solution. However, I also admit that at the time I was skeptical that yet another green, sustainable certification was being introduced and wondered if it would get any real traction in the crowded market for certifications.

In hindsight, it is clear that my concerns were unfounded. B Labs and their B Corp Certification have gained significant legitimacy in the global sustainability community. At the time of writing, there are more than 2,000 certified B Corps in dozens of countries around the globe. What makes B Corp so unique to the myriad of other certification schemes is that

firms who attain and retain B Corp status make a legally binding commitment (when countries or territories allow for this; if not, they must amend
their governing documents to codify their commitments) to some form
of Benefit Corporation legal status in their countries, voluntarily obligat-
ing them to meet very high levels of sustainability (social and ecological)
across all of their operations. For the first several years, most certified B
Corps were smaller, entrepreneurial firms; however, in recent years, even
some multinational, publicly traded firms have gone through the arduous
process of changing their incorporation to comply to the B Corp standards,
such as Natura (Brazil), Etsy (New York), and Silver Chef (Australia).

The fact that there are publicly traded certified B Corps might suggest
that these companies are firmly entrenched in neoliberal capitalist interpretations of organizing and that I should not have included a chapter on B
Corps and more broadly the idea of Benefit Corporations in a book about
post-capitalist entrepreneurship. Yet, as I indicated in the introduction to
this book, I consider Benefit Corporations as an interesting transitionary
model toward PCE. Benefit Corporations are incorporated with a legally
binding mandate to adhere to broader societal impact well beyond profit
maximization for shareholders. I should clarify that B Corps and B Corp
Certifications are those administered by the B Labs Foundation, while
Benefit Corporations represent any company who has incorporated as a
Benefit Corporation in a state or jurisdiction that supports this organizational form. Therefore, it is possible to be legally designated as a Benefit
Corporation and not be a certified B Corp, and in some cases the reverse
is true, particularly in jurisdictions that still do not have a legal form of
Benefit Corporation.

Wikipedia's introduction to Benefit Corporations summarizes this
nicely:

> In the United States, a Benefit Corporation is a type of for-profit corpo-
> rate entity, authorized by 30 U.S. states and the District of Columbia that
> includes positive impact on society, workers, the community and the
> environment in addition to profit as its legally defined goals. Benefit corpo-
> rations differ from traditional C corporations in purpose, accountability,
> and transparency, but not in taxation. Since December 2015, the Italian
> Parliament has introduced a new type of for-profit corporate entity named
> Società Benefit, a virtual translation of the US form, thus making Italy the
> first country in the world to make this legal status available on its entire
> territory. Australia is in the process of drafting their own, similar, version,
> as of February 2016.[3]

B CORP CASE STUDIES

Ben & Jerry's

Ben & Jerry's is not a startup anymore. Nor is it a firm with a heavy reliance on technology like much of the projects discussed in this book. But, it represents a great case study of a B Corp which has fully ingrained purpose into the organization. In a recent interview, Ben & Jerry's current CEO, Jostein Solheim, articulated how focused the fair trade ice cream company is on their purpose mandate:

> "We're a social justice company that happens to sell ice cream. Not the other way around. Our whole motto is how we can positively impact society."[4]

Ben & Jerry's path to becoming a B Corp is quite unique in the sense that Ben & Jerry's was founded way before the concept of B Corp was introduced. It is also a fascinating case because Ben & Jerry's became a B Corp after being acquired by the multinational conglomerate, Unilever, making Ben & Jerry's the first (and perhaps still only) wholly owned subsidiary to obtain B Corp certification.

> As a wholly owned subsidiary of Unilever, the B Corp certification may even be a bit sweeter. When Ben & Jerry's was acquired, many folks thought it would be a challenge for the company to keep its values. We're thrilled to join the movement. To undergo the process of certification, where every facet of our business is scrutinized to ensure that we're walking the talk, is rigorous but rewarding. It allows an experienced, holistic, values-led third party entity that B Lab is the chance to affirm that we remain true to our mission and look to accelerate our social impact. (Solheim in *The Guardian*[5])

And once they obtained B Corp status, the founders of B Corp were ecstatic as well, given that Ben & Jerry's is commonly credited with inspiring the Benefit Corporation and B Labs Foundation.

> "It's awesome to have Ben & Jerry's join a movement that they inspired." (Jay Coen Gilbert).[6]

Let's go back to the beginning of Ben & Jerry's, when in fact, it was a startup.*

---

* For this case study, I have drawn significantly from a research article I published with Pablo Muñoz in 2017 in the *California Management Review*, entitled: Entering Consious Consumer Markets.

In 1978, childhood friends Ben Cohen and Jerry Greenfield scraped together $8,000 and secured a $4,000 bank loan in order to convert an old gas station into an ice cream parlor in Burlington, Vermont. With unusually named flavors like Cherry Garcia and Chunky Monkey, combined with natural and unique ingredients, and a distinctive corporate culture with a values-based mission focused on community impact, Ben & Jerry's gained quick market acceptance. In 1984, Ben & Jerry's growth led them to launch an initial public offering (IPO). By 1992, sales reached $132 million and by 1999, annual sales of Ben & Jerry's ice cream climbed to nearly $240 million.

Not surprisingly, Ben & Jerry's demonstration of a market opportunity for unique flavors and responsible ice cream made the company an acquisition target. In late 1999, Unilever, on a mission to supplant Nestle as America's Ice Cream King, began courting Ben & Jerry's for future acquisition. Yet, the founders had major reservations about a multinational company with virtually no prior experience as a socially conscious leader taking over responsibility for the company they had carefully cultivated into a household name for both the quality and diversity of their ice cream and their absolute dedication to socially responsible principles.

Ben & Jerry's has had social responsibility and fair trade principles embedded into its mission from the beginning, before those terms were even being used in the industry. Their mission as defined on the company website includes three interrelated components. Socially, they seek to operate the company in a way that actively recognizes the central role that business plays in society by initiating innovative ways to improve the quality of life locally, nationally, and internationally. In terms of their products, Ben & Jerry's aims to make, distribute, and sell the finest quality of natural ice cream with a continued commitment to incorporating wholesome, natural ingredients and promoting business practices that respect the earth and the environment. Finally, in economic terms, they seek to operate the company on a sustainable financial basis of profitable growth, increasing value for stakeholders and expanding opportunities for development and career growth for their employees.[7]

During the negotiations, Ben Cohen and Jerry Greenfield pushed Unilever hard on issues of independence for the Ben & Jerry's brand, including an independent board and a binding commitment to maintaining their ingrained social values and community programming which had helped define the company since its founding. After much wrangling, a deal was finally achieved. In April of 2000, Unilever purchased Ben & Jerry's for $326 million, agreeing to allow the new subsidiary to have a board independent of Unilever.

Despite reported early struggles in the transition under Unilever ownership, Ben & Jerry's has managed to maintain its commitment to social responsibility. In 2010, the company announced plans to achieve 100% certified fair trade for all of their ice cream flavors in the United States by 2013. Ben & Jerry's became the first ice cream maker in the world to use Fairtrade-certified ingredients. In 2015, Ben & Jerry's paid $1,895,778 in social premiums to low-income producers in Ghana, Ivory Coast, Uganda, Mexico, Ecuador, and Belize.

Interestingly, Unilever is reportedly considering seeking B Corp status for the entire corporation which would make Unilever only the second publicly traded corporation to commit to the requirements of B Corp certification. As such, Unilever has agreed to work with the B Corp organization B Lab to support the adoption of B Corp by other publicly traded multinationals.[8]

Peerby

We now turn our attention toward a more modern case, Peerby, founded in 2011 in Amsterdam by Eelke Boezeman and Daan Weddepohl. Peerby from the beginning was a different kind of startup, despite participating in a traditional tech startup accelerator, Techstars, and having raised subsequent funding from venture capitalists. Peerby's founders did not start the company with a goal of profiting from transactions between peers, but instead for facilitating the optimization of underutilized resources and the creation of community by enabling neighbors to share common household items with each other for free. One could argue that the core Peerby model is a commons-based platform not for peer production as discussed in Chapter 1, but rather as a platform for sharing existing underutilized resources. In 2015, Peerby became one of the first sharing-economy companies to become a certified B Corp. While some have referred to Peerby as a platform cooperative,[9] the subject of Chapter 4, Peerby is really a hybrid model of sharing somewhere between platform capitalism and platform cooperative. For example, Peerby's new revenue-generating service, Peerby Go, facilitates access to similar household goods as their traditional free-sharing model, but in exchange for rental fees, Peerby offers added value features including curated products, delivery, and insurance. Regardless of how we might try to define their business model, Peerby is definitely an example of purpose-driven B Corp with a mission to increase social cohesion in the neighborhoods where peers exchange household items while also curbing climate change by reducing consumption and waste.[10]

B Corps for Startups

While the B Corp certification program serves as an aspirational goal to many entrepreneurs, the B Labs Foundation requires all startups to have at least 12 months of operating experience prior to seeking certification. However, recently, responding to growing demand from early-stage startups, B Labs introduced a new designation entitled "Certification Pending" for startups less than 12 months in existence. The benefits for the Certification Pending status are:

> You get to use the nifty Certification Pending logo. This can be useful to communicate to all your stakeholders (e.g. investors, employees, customers, retail or other business partners) that you are on the path to full B Corp Certification, which Inc. has called "the highest standard for socially responsible businesses."

You also get to engage as a soon-to-be B Corp peer with a community of more than 1,000 Certified B Corps to help you build a better business as you move to full certification. They'll know you're different from all other startups looking for a little love because you've already met the legal requirement for full certification and committed to meeting the performance requirement in the next 12 months.[11]

At the time of writing, B Labs Foundation asked startups seeking pending status to meet the legal requirements (either incorporating as a Benefit Corporation in their state or jurisdiction, if available, or amend the governing documents) and to complete a B Impact Assessment

> that envisions the positive impact the business intends to create through its business and operations as of the first anniversary of earning Pending status.

I had a chance to meet with German Cuenca, a founder of a B Corp Pending startup called Ethikos. Ethikos aims to be "the ethical alternative in people management" by connecting "good people with good companies." Ethikos was the first startup in Spain to obtain B Corp Pending status. They offer recruitment, training, and coaching, and outsourced human resource consulting. Currently they have 35 clients and a handful of employees. They reinvest 10% of their revenues in local nonprofits and offer their services for free to low-income individuals seeking employment. In early 2017, they "graduated" from pending status to B Corp certified and appear to be on their way to success.

Yet, before you commit to the B Corp Pending Certification model if you are in the early stages of a startup, it is important to reflect on the implications of locking into this model at such an early stage.

Research on 14 B Corp–Certified Companies

Along with my colleagues, Pablo Muñoz and Gabriel Caccioti, we decided to research entrepreneurs who had pursued B Corp certification in order to understand how they actually integrate purpose into the enterprise. Specifically, we interviewed founders of 14 different B Corp–certified startups about the process they went through to embed purpose into their organization over time. All of the firms we interviewed are based in Latin America (which is where two of us were living when we began conducting the research. From Chile, we interviewed founders of a food startup, a solar panel producer, and a bottled water producer; from Argentina, we interviewed an ethical fashion founder; and from Colombia, a fair trade coffee producer among others.

We found three factors affected how a commitment to purpose shapes (and is shaped by) the company and founders over time: (1) scope of purpose, (2) timing of when the startup obtained B Corp certification, and (3) interactions with the market and the media. I will summarize these factors and then introduce a typology we discovered of different B Corp models that emerged.

1. Scope of purpose. Some of the B Corp entrepreneurs we interviewed had vague notions of their purpose. We found that some B Corp founders started their ventures with very abstract ideas about having some kind of social impact. For example, a B Corp founder in the health sector stated:

   So, we wanted to tackle an important social problem, because I graduated with the desire to change the world.

Whereas other B Corp founders expressed a more concrete framing of their purpose:

> We started exporting organic food products ... while we were growing, we detected massive inequalities in the industry's purchasing model where the farmers are left behind. Then we developed a new purchasing model ("co-responsibility"), to empower coffee producers.

Founders with more concrete purposes also have more tangible metrics to confirm their impact. The same founder from a Colombian-based fair trade coffee company:

> We went from 9,000 to 30,000 bags of certified coffee beans in 3 years, which has enabled us to make a great work with the farmers... we are convinced of the (relevance of) the certification processes, the impacts that we have achieved through the certifications, in the farming communities, through the purchase of certified coffee, through a higher income. A certified coffee today represents an additional 35% in income for the farmer compared to non-certified coffee.

2. Timing of certification. For an entrepreneur aspiring to change the world, one might assume that achieving a certification such as B Corp early in the process makes a lot of sense. It gives a clear signal to all current and future stakeholders that this is not a traditional neoliberal enterprise focused on profit maximization and perhaps a quick sale of the company to a larger one. We discovered a range of choices made by entrepreneurs regarding when they opted for B Corp certification. Whereas some did so as soon as they were eligible (12 months of operation), others came to B Corp later, sometimes as a result of embracing purpose, not at founding, as they evolved their enterprise.
3. Interactions with the market and the media. The third factor of differentiation among B Corp founders is how they react to different signals of legitimacy. Some focus more on how the market (i.e., their customers) reacts to the firm's offerings. For example, one B Corp entrepreneur in our sample targeting ethical fashion in Paris expressed her evolving interaction with the market and refining the business model as a result:

> There was a lot of trial and error, of experimenting. We started growing, little by little, attending sustainable fashion shows, Ethical Fashion Show in Paris, Ethical Fashion Forum, Green Show... we opened new

> luxury markets in Europe, slowly, it was difficult but there was some
> willingness to pay for sustainable fashion…the trend was growing…
> then we received investment and opened our first small shop in Paris…
> then the crisis in Europe, purchasing decisions changed and we moved
> part of it to USA, with e-commerce, marketing, many things.

Meanwhile, other founders seem to be more impacted by legitimacy signals from the media. We found this to be particularly true for B Corp founders whose businesses had some struggle to achieve market traction. When faced with financial difficulties, some B Corp founders sought or latched onto other forms of legitimacy as a way of maintaining the strength to keep the enterprise moving forward:

> Then it is like when you are about to lower your arms, suddenly there is a
> good news about (the company), it like an adrenaline injection that gets
> you back convinced that we will get there. (Founder of a recycling company
> in Argentina).

What was really interesting after analyzing all of the interview data and comparing the 14 founders is how each founder addresses the three factors discussed above, we recognized patterns emerging from the interview data. This led to the creation of three different typologies of B Corp enterprises (Figure 2.1).

Type 1. Type 1 B Corps had abstract purposes, tended to have lower early market traction, leading them to focus on nonmarket signals of legitimacy (like media attention). Type 1 B Corps also tended to obtain B Corp certification earlier in their development and before they had discovered a functioning business model. As many of the entrepreneurs were operating in locations where there were few B Corps, these Type 1 founders were able to take advantage of this unique position to garner more media attention. Yet, the lack of a concrete purpose and market validation lead Type 1 ventures to experience financial problems, leading to disputes among the founding team members regarding the firm's commitment to purpose and their business model.

Type 2. Interestingly, Type 2 B Corps were not even purpose-driven when they founded the firm. Type 2 founders started their enterprises based on a business opportunity and more quickly sought market validation (as opposed to a focus on media). Yet, as the firm evolved, for several reasons including market demand, Type 2 ventures begin to embrace a concrete purpose and then seek B Corp certification to solidify their

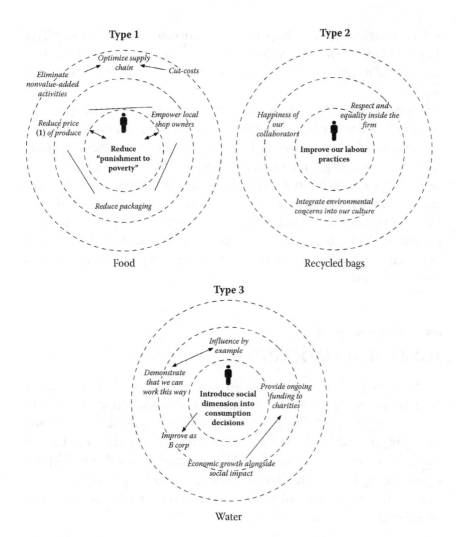

FIGURE 2.1
Typologies of B Corp enterprises (a) Food, (b) Recycled bags, and (c) Water. (From working paper submitted to the *Journal of Business Venturing* with Pablo Muñoz and Gabriel Cacciotti.)

commitment to purpose, recognizing B Corp certification as beneficial to their business objectives while increasingly showing an authentic commitment to purpose.

Type 3. Type 3 B Corps are a very unique breed and one that we hadn't anticipated discovering. Type 3 founders were committed to being part of a social movement. Type 3 founders were not necessarily concerned about starting a company at all. The company is really for them just a vehicle to achieve their bold goals to be part of an important change in society. Type 3 founders were willing to evolve their business model numerous times in the hope of discovering one that allows them to achieve the impact they aspire to.

So what can we learn from this research for aspiring B Corps entrepreneurs? A few key lessons emerge. First, it is important for B Corps to not lock in purpose too early through B Corp certification. Lean startup methodology, for example, suggests that entrepreneurs are in search of a repeatable business model and that founders should not commit to the first one they identify. This requires back and forth with early adopters to gain insights to refine the business model. If an entrepreneur seeks B Corp certification before he has identified the repeatable business model, we discovered this leads to premature lock-in of the social mission.

FOR-BENEFIT ASSOCIATIONS

Aside from for-benefit-incorporated companies, which I consider to be a transitional or hybrid organizational model between for-profit enterprising, market-based enterprising, and post-capitalist enterprising, an organizational model more aligned with post-capitalism is the for-benefit association. In the words of Michel Bauwens and Vasilis Kostakis, by connecting CBPP from Chapter 1 and for-benefit approaches from this chapter, for-benefit associations are pushing the envelope of alternative organizing.

> Many CBPP ecosystems not only consist of productive communities and entrepreneurial coalitions, but also have separate governance institutions that support the infrastructure of cooperation and, thus, empower the capacity for CBPP. Though they (for-benefit associations) often take the form of nonprofits, they do not command and direct the CBPP processes itself.[12]

Bauwens and Kostakis refer to the Wikimedia Foundation as a primary example of for-benefit associations. The Wikimedia Foundation is a nonprofit charity which survives mostly on the donations of time and money from the global community who support their goal for a world "in which every single human being can freely share in the sum of all knowledge."

While the Wikimedia Foundation does not coerce knowledge creators to commit to the values of open and free knowledge sharing, it does create the platform for such sharing and distribution for a range of content creation and sharing sites, Wikipedia of course being the most prominent. At the time of writing, there were 16 initiatives officially under the Wikimedia Foundation umbrella, all of which commit to a Creative Commons license and all supported projects can be "freely used, edited, copied, and redistributed, subject to the terms of the license." Some of the initiatives developed by the Foundation include Wiktionary (multilingual dictionary), Wikibooks (ebooks and textbooks), Wikiversity (learning materials and communities), and Wikimedia Incubator which facilitates the development of new projects in the Foundation. There are also dozens or possibly hundreds of other knowledge-sharing platforms which have leveraged the open source MediaWiki software which was not actually developed by the Foundation.

> For-benefit associations operate from a point of view of abundance... maintaining an infrastructure of cooperation that allows contributive communities and entrepreneurial coalitions to engage in CBPP processes vital for solving these issues. Not only do they protect these commons through licenses, but may also help manage conflicts between participants and stakeholders, fundraise, and assist in the general capacity building necessary for the commons in particular fields of activity.[12]

CONCLUSION

Benefit corporations, including the rapid growth of the B Corp movement, show promise as a transitionary organizing model for for-profit enterprises seeking to ensure that profit maximization does not take precedence over social and ecological impacts. While there is a growing interest in B Corps from a startup perspective, and the B Lab Foundation is trying to allow for early-stage startups to join the club, my research with colleagues suggests that the timing of when a founder commits to his or her purpose is important and that it is possible committing early can be detrimental to the firm and their aspired future impact. Benefit Associations, usually nonprofit, are more aligned with what the PCE paradigm espouses in this book and provide a link between commons thinking and platform cooperatives, the focus of Chapter 3.

REFERENCES

1. Nathan Bomey, BP's Deepwater Horizon Costs $62B, *USA Today*, July 2016. http://www.usatoday.com/story/money/2016 07/14/bp-deepwater-horizon-costs/ 87087056/ (accessed October 2016).
2. Alexandra Adams, *Summary of Information concerning the Ecological and Economic Impacts of the BP Deepwater Horizon Oil Spill Disaster*, NRDC Issue Paper, NRDC, Washington, D.C. June 2015.
3. Benefit Corporation, Wikipedia, https://en.wikipedia.org/wiki/ Benefit_ corporation#cite_note-1 (accessed November 2016).
4. Aaron Hurst, Why Ben and Jerry's Pushes his Company to Merge Ice Cream and Social Justice, *Fast Company*, January 2017, https://www.fastcoexist.com/3067597/ thepurposeful-ceo/why-ben-and-jerrys-ceo-pushes-his-company-to-merge-ice-creamand-social-j (accessed February 2017).
5. Jo Confino, Will Unilever become the world's largest publicly traded B Corp? *The Guardian*, January 23, 2015, https://www.theguardian.com/sustainablebusiness/2015/ jan/23/benefit-corporations-bcorps-business-social-responsibility (accessed February 16, 2016).
6. Anne Field, Ben & Jerry's Poster Child for the B Corp Movement, Becomes a B Corp, Forbes, October, 2012. http://www.forbes.com/sites/annefield/2012/10/22/ben-jerrys-poster-child-for-the-b-corp-movement-becomes-a-b-corp/#7e311903511e (accessed May 2016).
7. Ben & Jerry's Social Responsibility page, http://bjsocialresponsibility.weebly.com (accessed May 2016).
8. M. Gunther, Can B Corp be the Next Fair Trade for Socially-Minded Corporations? *The Guardian*, January 7, 2016. https://www.theguardian.com/sustainablebusiness/2016/ jan/07/b-corp-leed-fair-trade-certification-sustainability-lab-danonegroup-black-rock-unilever (accessed April 2016).
9. Cat Johnson, 11 Platform Cooperatives Creating a Real Sharing Economy, *P2P Foundation*, https://blog.p2pfoundation.net/11-platform-cooperatives-creatingreal-sharing-economy/2016/06/01 (accessed June 2016).
10. Peerby Homepage, http://press.peerby.com/ (accessed March 2017).
11. B Corporation Homepage, https://www.bcorporation.net/become-a-b-corp/how-to-become-a-b-corp/steps-start-ups (accessed April 2017).
12. M. Bauwens and V. Kostakis, A new post-capitalist ecosystem of value creation, *Open Democracy*, January 7, 2017. https://www.opendemocracy.net/michel - bauwens-vasilis-kostakis/new-post-capitalist-ecosystem-of-value-creation (accessed January 2017).

3

From the Platform Deathstars to Technology-Enabled Platform Cooperativism

INTRODUCTION TO COOPERATIVES

Cooperative forms of organizing have coexisted with more traditional profit-driven enterprise in market economies for decades. Yet, cooperatives are fundamentally different in that their ownership and governance model is distributed across the members. Instead of private ownership over labor and the means of production, cooperatives aim to share the wealth and responsibilities among member/owners. "Cooperatives are autonomous associations of people united voluntarily to meet their common economic, social and cultural needs and aspirations through a jointly owned and democratically controlled business."[1]

Cooperatives exist across most sectors of the economy, including cooperative credit unions, housing cooperatives, consumer cooperatives, producer cooperatives, and worker cooperatives. In aggregate, cooperatives are already a significant part of the global economy. Global membership in cooperatives exceeds 1 billion people in 96 countries.[2] Even in advanced economies, cooperatives often represent a significant amount of economic activity, such as Finland (21%) and New Zealand (17.5%). More than 1,400 cooperatives worldwide generate more than 100 million in annual revenue, and in 2014, the 300 largest cooperatives generated a combined $2.5 billion (USD) in revenue.[3] While many cooperatives are small and local, even before technology allowed for potentially infinite scalability of this alternative organizational form, some cooperatives have managed to scale not just nationally but regionally or even globally.

MONDRAGON

Widely considered the largest worker cooperative in the world, with $15.7 billion (USD) in revenues and nearly 75,000 worker members, Mondragon Group got its start from humble beginnings. In 1956, a Catholic priest, Jose Maria Arizmendiarrieta inspired five of his students at a technical college in the town of Mondragon to establish a local workers cooperative called Talleres Ulgor. The original group continued to help, support, and spin out new forms of worker and consumer cooperatives over the following years and decades. Today, Mondragon has more than 250 different cooperatives under its umbrella across four sectors: finance, manufacturing, education, and distribution. Thus, Mondragon has been able to achieve an impact far and wide, and it has also ensured an everlasting impact on its home community in the Basque region of Spain. Barbara Peters, a retired professor and poverty expert from Long Island University, experienced Mondragon, the town in 2000 and came away impressed:

> In Mondragon, I saw no signs of poverty. I saw no signs of extreme wealth. I saw people looking out for each other. It's a caring form of capitalism. It's profit-making, but the workers make the profit. They buy into it, and can get loans to do so from a cooperative bank. ... My recent trip there was just incredible.[4]

While the cooperative model has a long track record over several decades, very recently, the concept of platform cooperatives emerged to enable a different type of sharing, powered by a platform, with cooperative ownership structures offering an alternative to the mainstream, venture-capital-backed platform capitalist models of the sharing economy. The rest of this chapter is dedicated to exploring the evolution of platform cooperatives and highlighting their potential in a post-capitalist entrepreneurship (PCE) society.

PLATFORM COOPERATIVES

We have witnessed a rapid growth in the use of platforms for connecting peers and businesses to each other. While this has been labeled as the sharing economy, many sharing enterprises have been accused of exploitative behavior and damaging, rather than improving communities. Airbnb, Uber, Deliveroo, and others have been sued and even banned in countries around the globe for skirting regulation and exploiting "independent contractors" who are really employees without minimum wages, benefits, or health care. This has given the sharing economy and its entrepreneurs a bad name. In fact, some, such as Shareable's Neal Gorenflo, refer to them as Platform Deathstars, referencing Darth Vader's battleship in Star Wars. Generally, I refer to Airbnb, Uber, and the like as platform capitalism. Since this book is about post-capitalist entrepreneurship, my objective with this chapter is to focus on the antithesis, a movement generally referred to as platform cooperatives.

Before diving into the specifics of different business models and platform cooperatives, it may be useful to put the sharing economy in a broader context. A couple of my colleagues, Duncan McClaren and Julian Agyeman, published a great book *Sharing Cities* in 2016 not only to frame the sharing economy as a primarily urban phenomenon but also to clarify the range of sharing activities that have occurred in society throughout time. One particular graphic from that book is informative and helps to put this chapter in context of the other chapters and the broader thinking on the collaborative or sharing economy.

As you can see, there are different dimensions of sharing activities. McClaren and Agyeman refer to this broader framing as the sharing paradigm whereby the very commercial, platform capitalist models fall within the bottom left quadrant (Figure 3.1). Sharing that relates to the commons falls in the top two quadrants of their sharing paradigm model. While commons-based peer production (the subject of Chapter 1) is in the top right quadrant, platform cooperatives would fall into the top left quadrant. For me, one of the distinguishing features of platform cooperatives with commons-based peer production (CBPP) is that platform cooperatives more frequently are about facilitating access to resources already produced, whereas CBPP is generally about creating networks of coproduction and co-consumption.

There are thousands of sharing economy projects, some technology enabled and some no or low-tech, which have embraced more of a commons approach to sharing, although they generate much less media attention than the deathstars. In this chapter, I will introduce the Sharing Business Model Compass and Sharing Business Model Canvas I developed with my colleague Pablo Muñoz after researching dozens of sharing-economy business models and introduce the growth

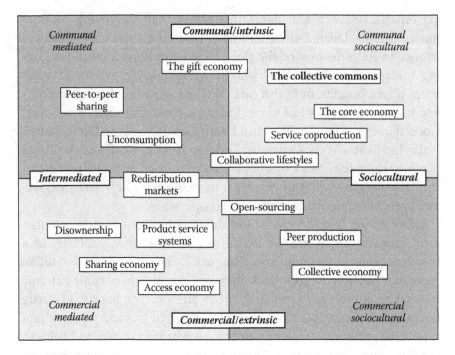

FIGURE 3.1
Sharing Paradigm, reprinted with permission, *Sharing Cities: A Case for Truly Smart and Sustainable Cities*, by Duncan McLaren and Julian Agyeman, published by The MIT Press.

of platform cooperatives as an interesting alternative approach to the creation of sharing economy enterprises.

Business Models of Platform Cooperatives

Two colleagues I have interacted with on several occasions, Trebor Scholz and Nathan Schneider, are widely credited with introducing and building a movement for platform cooperatives (platform coops). The movement started to coalesce around the first conference about platform coops they hosted in New York in 2015. As they suggest in their recent book *The Rise of Platform Cooperativism, A New Vision for the Future of Work and a Fairer Internet:*

> Combining the rich heritage of cooperatives with the promise of 21st-century technologies, platform cooperativism is a call for a new kind of online economy, one free from the economics of monopoly, exploitation, and surveillance.[5]

The peer-to-peer (P2P) Foundation, the most influential sharing and commons-based economy wiki site, founded by Michel Bauwens, defines platform coops as:

> worker-owned cooperatives designing their own apps-based platforms, fostering truly peer-to-peer ways of providing services and things.

If the deathstars, or platform capitalists, are one extreme, and platform coops are on the other, then what differentiates these two extremes and what makes up all the gray area in the middle? To begin to get under the hood of the business models of sharing-economy players and to answer these questions, my colleague, Pablo Muñoz, and I analyzed hundreds of sources of data on 36 different sharing business startups representative of Jeremiah Owyang's Honeycomb model, a graphical depiction of the different sectors where sharing startups have gained traction.

While the Honeycomb model has been of great use in framing the diversity of sectors being impacted or disrupted by the sharing economy, it does not provide any insights on the underlying business models across the 12 different sharing-economy sectors that Owyang identifies in his Honeycomb v2.0. The sectors included learning, municipal, money, goods, health and wellness, space, food, utilities, transportation, services, logistics, and corporates. Since we completed our research, Owyang released his 3.0 version which included four more sectors, demonstrating how fast the sharing space is growing.

After in-depth analysis, Pablo and I identified six key dimensions of sharing economy business models, each of them with three distinct decisions that can be made by sharing startups. We converted this into the Sharing Business Model Compass.

SHARING BUSINESS MODEL COMPASS*

Four of the six dimensions of the Sharing Business Model Compass—transaction, business approach, governance model, and platform type—offer business model decision choices roughly on a continuum from more

---

* This chapter, in particular, this section about the Compass includes content from my Fast Company and Shareable.net posts about the compass, as well as content from the academic research I did with Pablo Muñoz.

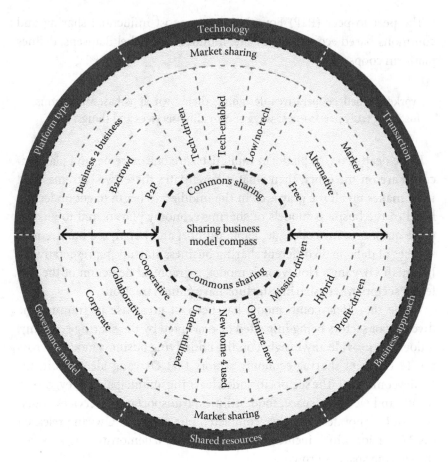

FIGURE 3.2

Sharing Business Model Compass by Boyd Cohen and Pablo Muñoz.

market-based sharing (i.e., platform capitalism) toward commons-based sharing (i.e., platform cooperatives). The other two dimensions—technology and shared resources—have decisions relatively agnostic to market or commons orientations. What I mean here is that with respect to technology and shared resources, we were unable to determine a continuum. We found platform capitalists using little technology and platform coops relying heavily on technology and similar deviations with respect to resources (Figure 3.2).

Technology

Within this dimension, there are three choices: tech-driven, tech-enabled, and low/no-tech. Tech-driven business models are those leveraging technology not just to connect users but also to complete the transaction without the need for offline interaction. Crowdfunding sites like Kickstarter and Indiegogo and online learning portals such as Udacity and Coursera fall in the tech-driven category. The majority of the startups we studied fall more in the tech-enabled category, which represents business models reliant on technology to facilitate the connections but require or are enhanced by offline interactions. Wallapop, a fast-growing hyper-local mobile classified business for P2P reselling of used goods would fall into this category. While most of what we think about in the sharing-economy space is at least enabled by technology, there are still many startups in the sharing space where technology is at most a supporting tool but not critical (i.e., low/no-tech). Co-working spaces and shared commercial kitchens are good examples of the low/no-tech business model, while other models such as the Repair Café are hyper-local, nonprofit, no-tech sharing actors. Of course, these low-tech models do not scale in the same way as digitally enabled ones and are generally not considered part of the platform coop movement.

Transaction

We observed three variations in transaction types: market, alternative, and free. Perhaps the most extreme version of market transaction is Uber, which does not only vary pricing based on demand but also includes the highly controversial surge pricing. Most of the scaled, venture-capital-backed platform capitalist projects—such as Airbnb and Rent the Runway—opt for market pricing. The alternative option is just starting to emerge. While there are perhaps fewer scaled examples so far, Bliive, a rapidly globalizing time bank out of Brazil, is a good example (discussed in Chapter 4). Yerdle, a P2P service for exchanging used goods also falls into the alternative category. Instead of exchange for cash, users earn Yerdle dollars for acquiring other goods in the future. Peerby, another P2P used goods exchange, founded in Amsterdam in 2011, offers a completely free service. Of course, many bike-sharing services are free or just require an annual deposit. While you may think that free bike-sharing services have no business model, and perhaps are just subsidized public transit options, think again. Most of the scaled bike-sharing services in cities like Paris, Mexico City, London, and New York City generate revenue through sponsorships or advertising models.

Business Approach

There are three primary options from sharing providers with respect to the business approach: profit-driven, hybrid, and mission-driven. We consider Uber, Upwork, and eBay to be among the many sharing platforms that are profit-driven. Hybrid models are those that are usually founded as for-profits but have a clearly stated goal that drives them to create social and/or environmental benefits in communities. Zipcar, sold to Avis for $500 million, is a good example as it was founded and stayed true to the goal of reducing congestion and contamination in cities, while providing access to a vehicle for people who could not afford or chose not to own one (or a second) vehicle. Kickstarter, at a minimum, would also be considered a hybrid approach as they aspire to support creative projects around the globe and to be good corporate citizens. At the end of 2014, Kickstarter joined the growing group of responsible companies who became a certified B Corp (discussed in Chapter 2). Kiva is even further down the path of a mission-driven company, having formed as "a nonprofit organization with a mission to connect people through lending to alleviate poverty." Certainly, the more than 1,200 Repair Cafes around the globe would fit squarely in the mission-driven category as well.

Shared Resources

In her book, *Peers, Inc.*, Robin Chase (the founder of Zipcar) suggested that sharing business models optimize under-utilized resources in society. We agree, although as we studied the business models we realized that there are really three ways sharing startups seek to achieve this. They optimize new resources, help find a new home for used resources, or facilitate the optimization of under-utilized, existing resources. Zipcar itself is a good example of the optimization of new resources as more often than not their fleet is made up entirely of newly acquired vehicles. Rent the Runway actually started with a model focused on the optimization of under-utilized existing resources (e.g., dresses worn once to a wedding) but have shifted their model in recent years to the optimization of new resources where the company acquires new clothing for rental to users of their platform. Many of the P2P models for used items already mentioned (e.g., Wallapop, eBay, Peerby) fall into the "new home for used resources" category. In the optimization of under-utilized resources category, P2P car sharing and carpooling models like Blablacar fit well. Similarly, crowd-shipping models such as Shipizy also belong here.

Governance Model

The governance models for sharing startups range significantly, from traditional corporate structures to collaborative governance models to cooperative models. This of course is one of the categories that most directly distinguishes platform capitalism from platform cooperativism. Corporate structures seem to be the choice, not surprising, for most venture-capital-backed business models in the sharing economy (e.g., Uber, Airbnb, Upwork, Rent the Runway). Add in how many of the platform capitalist firms have embraced the three-class share structure, popularized by Google, which gives the founders 10 times the voting rights of other shareholders, and you can see that collaborative governance, even with internal shareholders, is not on the agenda for the profit-driven sharing platforms.[6]

Yet, some scaled sharing businesses such as Kiva embrace collaborative approaches to working with users and other stakeholders in sourcing, implementing, and monitoring projects funded through the platform. The cooperative governance model for sharing economy startups is only starting to take off. One pioneering and very successful platform cooperative is Stocksy, based in Victoria, Canada. Stocksy is a curated platform for obtaining high-quality photos and videos made by their artist community. Stocksy founded by visionary and passionate artist Brianna Wettlaufer has a strong commitment to collaborative governance and revenue sharing:

> We are an artist-owned cooperative founded on the principles of equality, respect, and fair distribution of profits. Our contributing artists receive 50% of a Standard License Purchase and 75% of an Extended License Purchase—and every single co-op member receives a share of the company...Stocksy is focused on the support and empowerment of sustainable artist careers through democratic business.[7]

In 2015, Stocksy, a pioneer in the platform coop movement, generated $7.9 million (USD) in revenues. Aside from the revenue sharing with the artists ($4.3 million (USD)), in 2015, Stocksy issued its first dividend to all its members. Of course, a coop this size has overhead in terms of servers, marketing, staffing, etc., but even so, well over half of revenues went straight to artist member's pockets.[8]

Platform Type

While we are used to thinking of the sharing economy as being P2P, in reality, there are at least three common platforms in use: business to business (B2B), business to crowd, and P2P. In the B2B category, you can find companies like Yardclub, founded by Caterpillar, which facilitates the rental of Caterpillar tractors for construction sites. Similarly, Cohealo facilitates the sharing of expensive hospital equipment between hospitals. In the business to crowd category, companies like Zipcar and Rent the Runway choose to own the resources that will be exchanged within the user community. And platforms where peers exchange products or services with each other, and where the platform provider owns virtually none of the shared assets (such as Indiegogo and Blablacar), fall into the classical P2P category. In general, we would expect to see more platform coops in the P2P space. This is true from our observation (i.e., there are very few platform coops that are not P2P); however, it is also true that several platform capitalists have opted for P2P platform models as well (e.g., Airbnb, Task Rabbit).

FROM PLATFORM COOP BUSINESS DIMENSIONS TO A SHARING BUSINESS MODEL CANVAS

Most entrepreneurs and those in the entrepreneurial community are well aware of the lean startup method. The lean startup methodology encourages founders to build empathy for potential users by employing design thinking and engaging in multiple experiments, referred to as minimum viable products (MVPs) in the hope of failing faster before discovering a solution that meets the needs of enough users with a revenue model that is sufficiently scalable to turn the idea into a real enterprise. One of the tools that is instrumental in applying the lean startup methodology is the Business Model Canvas, first introduced by Alexander Osterwälder. The original canvas contains nine different elements on just one page, allowing aspiring entrepreneurs to identify their guesses (referred to as hypotheses) about the fundamental aspects of their business model relating to the value proposition, revenue streams, partners, cost structure, and others. While the Business Model Canvas is very useful for traditional entrepreneurs, whereas it is less useful for post-capitalist entrepreneurs because the original canvas lacks a forced reflection on the impacts of the business model on communities. Several scholars and organizations have developed alternative versions of the canvas to reflect unique elements of business models in different sectors. For example, the Social Innovation Lab created an alternative canvas for social impact startups, called the Social Business Model Canvas.

Together with Pablo Muñoz we developed the Sharing-Economy Model Canvas, which emerged from the Compass discussed above. I have been employing it in my entrepreneurship courses at EADA in Barcelona for the past few years as the number of students interested in starting sharing enterprises has grown substantially since 2015 (Figure 3.3). As you can see, the canvas contains eight elements, including governance model, business approach, value proposition, shared resources, platform type, technology, cost structure, and transaction. As all of these elements are covered either above or in the vast literature on the canvas and lean startup, I will just focus here on our expanded view of technology. Instead of just understanding whether it is a tech-driven, enabled, or low-tech solution, we are also encouraging sharing entrepreneurs to reflect on their view of technology from an intellectual property perspective. As discussed in this chapter, and throughout this book, PCEs often have different motives beyond trying to monopolize a space and to maximize profit through

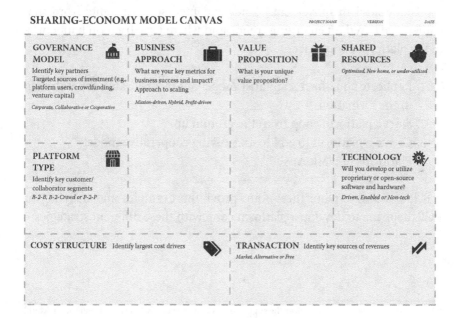

FIGURE 3.3
Sharing Business Model Canvas.

closed innovation. The range of open licensing models and examples from Chapter 1 are testament to the fact that PCEs may view technology more as a democratizing tool to support inclusive and sustainable development instead of a path to a billion dollar valuation and exit. While this does not rule out the possibility that we will see billion dollar PCEs, or at least transitionary models such as some of the B Corps discussed in Chapter 2 (e.g., Etsy, Natura), the commitment to the commons is almost universal among PCEs. So, reflecting on what technology a sharing platform might employ or develop is very important. PCEs may not only focus on developing technology which will embrace open licensing but also commit to only working with suppliers that utilize open licensing too.

SOURCES OF PLATFORM COOP OPPORTUNITIES

At the 2016 Platform Cooperativism conference, some clarity emerged regarding the different approaches through which post-capitalist entrepreneurs can merge the concept of platform economy with the values of the cooperativism movement.[9] I have adapted some insights from that conference based on emerging trends and where I see traction happening in the platform coop space:

1. Replicate a platform capitalist model but incorporate cooperativism in the formation
2. Start a platform coop from the ground up
3. Create a platform to add to an existing cooperative model
4. Platforms of platforms*

Below, I will explore these four, providing examples and insights for PCEs aspiring to develop a platform coop with these different strategies.

---

* In sharing these with Trebor Scholz, he suggested a more expanded list of transition models would include: (1) from the ground up, (2) from traditional cooperatives, (3) from academia, (4) from the corporate sector, (5) from failed VC funded startups and (6) platform of platforms.

Platform Coops as a Response to Platform Capitalism

There is a growing movement of technologically enabled "activists" who see platform coops as a potential direction response to the abuses of platform capitalists. I believe this model holds lots of potential. In part because many of the users who create value on these platforms are feeling exploited by the platform capitalists and are inspired to be part of an alternative. Also, if a model has proven successful as a platform-capitalist approach, than the private sector has essentially financed the validation of the business model, eliminating one of the most difficult barriers for startups. Many aspiring entrepreneurs dream of being first to market believing that gives them a better chance for success. But research has shown that more often than not, being a first mover is actually a disadvantage. The costs to educate and legitimize an entire population about a new model for doing things, and the challenges in learning how to best meet the needs in a new way, are both expensive and difficult for startups to accomplish.[10] Think about the Uber model for a minute. In hindsight, it was an obvious area ripe for disruption. The taxi industry was stuck in the 20th century with an old business model and virtually no technology enhancing the service for customers. But to scale a solution like Uber has required hundreds of billions of dollars, and has taken time to change user behavior and of course is still not legitimate in the eyes of many regulators. However, Uber is a very scaled enterprise that is changing an entire industry, while creating a lot of enemies, including taxi drivers.

One of my favorite stories regarding how a platform coop can emerge by mimicking a successful platform capitalist enterprise is with Green Taxi in Denver, Colorado. In response to growing demand from Uber, with the support of the Communication Workers of America, local taxi drivers in Denver decided to take matters into their own hands and to form their own platform cooperative. Each driver had to contribute $2,000 to be co-owners in the cooperative. In a short period of time, Green Taxi Cooperative became the largest individual taxi company in Denver, after 800 drivers from 37 different countries committed to the cause. Green Taxi Cooperative partnered with Autocab International to launch an app to compete with Uber in the Denver market. In a 2016 members meeting, Nathan Schneider was present to report on one of Green Taxi's early gatherings. Clearly, these coop members have quickly embraced their role as owners, where during one heated exchange about transparency in the coop's accounting, a coop member noted: *This is not just some job. This is our money and our company.* In this meeting, Jason Wiener, the lawyer for Green Taxi, spoke up trying to help the members understand the implications of this bold initiative: "What you're trying to do is not easy. Try to see the long arc here. You're starting a completely different way of organizing the economy and relating to the community."[11]

I believe we could easily see similar responses to a range of platform capitalist initiatives. Communities (physical or virtual) are increasingly emboldened by access to low-cost software solutions and a growing resistance movement to extreme, neoliberal approaches often leading more to value extraction. There are dozens if not more similar taxi cooperatives taking hold around the globe as a direct response to the threats posed by Uber along with a growing discontent among Uber's own drivers. Toward the end of 2016, Uber lost a lawsuit in the United Kingdom as it tried to continue its claim that Uber drivers are not employees and therefore not entitled to minimum wage or other employment benefits. Similarly, Deliveroo, a food delivery service, sought to also treat employees as independent contractors and also lost in court. As technology democratizes, and the 99% become increasingly disenfranchised, rather than just protest on the street, they are now taking matters into their own hands and creating alternative models that more fairly focus on value exchange instead of extraction.

It is only a matter of time before we see a proliferation of platform coops seeking to directly compete with platform capitalist enterprises. When the providers of real value (i.e., the driver, the laborer who does work on a Task Rabbit platform, etc.) join cooperative platforms, it will be increasingly difficult for platform capitalists to succeed in the long term. Of course, in the case of Uber, it is no secret that their long-term play is to shift to autonomous vehicles. In reality, Uber drivers today are really being used to validate Uber's business model and to improve Uber's algorithms so that they can automate out the drivers altogether. In fact, Uber has already begun testing an autonomous vehicle service in San Francisco despite it being against California regulations to do so without a permit.[12]

But, if you think of any extractive platform today, you can almost certainly envision how it could be challenged by a cooperative model. Why couldn't there be a platform coop version of Airbnb, for example? Where the owners of the units are actually owners of the platform and they share in the governance and the revenues on the platform. I had this conversation with Trebor Scholz during one of his recent visits to Barcelona. We both agreed that one angle for this could be for cities to regulate out Airbnb and to only authorize one platform to offer short-term rentals in their city and that could be some kind of city-sponsored or endorsed platform coop or even a blockchain-enabled distributed autonomous organization (see Chapter 5). Cities in a region, say Europe, could actually fund the software development in partnership to keep costs down and learn from each other. Then, cooperative teams in each city would gain access to the software, and perhaps using blockchain technology, embed the appropriate rules and regulations into the platform for each city.

For example, a few years ago, I had a conversation with a senior aid to Paris Mayor Ann Hidalgo where we discussed the city's struggles to get Airbnb to help enforce compliance to the French law that no housing units are allowed to be rented for short-term tourist use for more than 120 days in a year. There is no real reason Airbnb could not easily embed a code that notifies homeowners when they are approaching their maximum for the year and then automatically shut down that listing once their 120 days were reached. I was speaking at a Nesta conference in London about this and afterward I had a very angry Airbnb executive come up to me to inform me that since my discussion with the Paris city administrator, Airbnb had indeed advanced work with the city on this and that there were challenges I was not aware of in executing this. Regardless, the point is, the 120-day restriction could be embedded into a platform coop based on blockchain for any cities that wanted to implement it. The idea of a city or territory outlawing a platform capitalist is nothing new. In 2015, Uber was banned or partially banned in more than 10 countries around the world.

Platform Coop from the Ground Up

The Open Food Network UK (OFN UK), leveraging open-source software from the Open Food Foundation (founded in Australia), has developed a platform for supporting an ecosystem of producers, food stores, and food shoppers who are all committed to the cooperative values. The OFN UK was an initiative of four local food hubs throughout the United Kingdom who, in 2014, felt that if they combined forces they could improve their impact, sharing in the refinement of the

Open Food Network web platform. Since then the OFN UK has grown significantly, combining more than 250 producers, 40 shops, nearly 400 shoppers, and by February, 2017, completing more than 2,600 orders, growing the movement for local produce throughout the United Kingdom connected by an open cooperative platform. The OFN UK has committed to a set of nine key values that should all resonate with those interested in PCE: (1) global commons, (2) relationships, (3) local food ecosystems, (4) transparency, (5) empowerment, (6) subsidiarity (i.e., solving problems at the most local level possible), (7) people first, (8) constant evolution, and (9) systemic change. The OFN UK shows how collaboration for a common cause leveraging a platform coop model can be synergistic for the partners and the community. It also shows that platform coops are not only for facilitating the sharing of digital content but can also support new models of collaboration in traditional sectors like local food systems.

Fairmondo

Fairmondo was first founded in Germany in 2012 with the goal of becoming a global online marketplace cooperatively owned by its users in different countries around the globe. The German version of Fairmondo scaled quickly, reaching 2,000 members, 12,000 users offering more than 2 million products, including a range of fair-trade, sustainable items in multiple product categories. The German version of Fairmondo "is run by 12 part- and full-time members of the core team, including an executive board of 2 members, and is controlled by a 7-member supervisory board elected by co-op members."[13]

Fairmondo's vision of global expansion through localized cooperatives is gaining traction. Fairmondo UK was the first new addition to the Fairmondo platform cooperative model. Wherever Fairmondo expands, its local cooperatives must commit to the values established at the founding of Fairmondo in Germany, namely: (1) democratic ownership and organizational structure; (2) transparency, open source, and open innovation; (3) fair terms of collaboration; (4) clearly defined use of surplus (this refers to "profits" generated) and (5) promotion of responsible consumption. In its model of thinking locally and acting globally by supporting the proliferation of independent cooperatives in country expansions, Fairmondo offers a good transition to the next category I'd like to discuss: platforms of platforms.

Add a Platform to a Functioning Cooperative

Another option for the creation of new platform coops is to add a platform component to an existing cooperative model. Si Se Puede (yes we can in Spanish) is a women's cooperative committed to:

> create living wage jobs that will be carried out in a safe and healthy environment, and that promotes social supports and educational opportunities for its members.[14]

Si Se Puede was founded by 14 immigrant women in Brooklyn, New York, in 2006 to support themselves and other immigrant women (initially many Latin women) have a cooperatively owned housecleaning business. Similarly to the Denver taxi drivers who created Green Taxi, these women were inspired to find ways to improve living conditions by becoming co-owners of their own cooperative instead of being employees in a company. In 2015, at the first conference on Platform Cooperatives, Si Se Puede announced plans to shift toward a technologically enabled platform coop to expand their reach. In this case, the group is working "with a group of MBA candidates from Cornell Tech to develop an app that goes beyond just scaling the cooperative: it seeks to create a platform that elevates Si Se Puede! into the heights of the digital age, allowing them to offer home cleaning services to a wider spectrum of clients through a brand new customized smartphone app."[15]

AnyShare: The First FairShares Enterprise

Founded in Arizona by founders with tech startup experience, AnyShare is a platform cooperative designed to enable other groups and communities around the world to leverage AnyShare's software tools and governance model to form their own platform cooperatives. The founders of AnyShare grew disenchanted with capitalism as usual, having witnessed the extremes of profit maximizing from investors and the tech community inside a company which successfully issued an initial public offering.

> As time went on, I continued to learn about the extractive nature of business as usual and was attracted to the cooperative model. There were issues with cooperatives, in raising capital and not sharing the decision-making and value created with all the stakeholders that a technology-oriented business would impact. I began to imagine a hybrid cooperative that would create a business structure that would appease what had become a long list of requirements for me.[16]

AnyShare is a real pioneer in codifying a more holistic governance model for platform cooperatives. AnyShare is the first US cooperative to leverage FairShares multistakeholder cooperative governance model. FairShares itself is a cooperative and an organization dedicated to reframing enterprises in a way that embraces the values of the cooperative movement, allowing all stakeholders a voice and ownership in the enterprise. The FairShares multistakeholder governance model proposes bylaws which offer governance, ownership, and management control to four stakeholder groups: founders, investors, laborers, and customers. One of the reasons the founders of AnyShare embraced the FairShares model is that they saw it as a way to allow for external investors to participate in the funding and growth of AnyShare. This is a concern that the founders had with the cooperative model in that many cooperatives struggle with financing because they often rely on active members as their only source of capital.

AnyShares felt that one stakeholder group was absent, that of the natural environment, so they amended FairShares bylaws to include the environment as a separate stakeholder, to be represented by an individual on the board whose sole responsibility will be to focus on the environmental impact of AnyShare. Another amendment to the FairShares bylaws was made with respect to the commitment to registering all intellectual property with a Creative Commons license. AnyShare is fully committed to the values of the open commons movement, but they did not want to be restricted to just Creative Commons licenses. As discussed in Chapter 1, there are a growing number of open licenses and the founders of AnyShare wanted to maintain flexibility to choose the best and most appropriate license which allows them to achieve their organizational objectives.

Loomio, from Enspiral

The Enspiral Network was formed in 2010 in New Zealand as a collective to work toward incubating social enterprises. In 2011, a worker-owned cooperative was formed from members of the Enspiral Network in response to an observation from the Occupy Movement. As activists in the Occupy Movement struggled to coordinate their activities or to quickly reach decisions on next steps, it became apparent that software and Internet technologies could be put to service to solve the remote organizing needs of such regional and global movements. Loomio was formed as a cooperative to develop such tools and to make them accessible to activists around the globe. Loomio's team, led by Alanna Krause and Ben Knight, was able to first raise funds in a crowdfunding campaign and later with impact/ethical investors, to bring Loomio to the world. Much like Sharetribe (discussed in Chapter 1), Loomio offers a software as a service (SaaS) model, with free versions of their open-source software hosted on GitHub along with paid versions for larger groups or those seeking additional value-added services.

PLATFORMS OF PLATFORMS

Activists, technologists, and other citizen actors are starting to come together behind the platform cooperative movement in hopes of supporting like-minded individuals form their own platform coops. Practicing what they preach, FairCoop, Freedom Coop, and the Innovation Cooperative are three examples of what I would call platforms of platforms.

Perhaps one of the most influential, global platform coops is FairCoop. Their reach is far and wide and they are leaving no stone unturned in an effort to reshape the global economy away from capitalism and toward one that is people- and planet-friendly.

> Fair.coop is an open global cooperative, self-organized via the Internet and remaining outside nation-state control.
>
> Its aim is to make the transition to a new world by reducing the economic and social inequalities among human beings as much as possible, and at the same time gradually contribute to a new global wealth, accessible to all humankind as commons.[17]

In Chapter 4 on alternative currencies, I will introduce one of FairCoop's promising initiatives, FairCoin.

Freedom Coop

Freedom Coop is a "European Cooperative Society that creates toolkits for self-management, self-employment, economic autonomy, and financial disobedience for individuals and groups striving for fairer social and economic relationships." Essentially, Freedom Coop has created tools to facilitate the creation of other coops by anyone sharing their values whereby new coops can access Freedom Coops legal structures, free of charge, to get their own coops off the ground. Freedom Coop embraces the values of the open Internet, the commons, and alternative currencies as discussed in prior chapters. For example, Freedom Coop accepts membership fees in FairCoin, a cryptocurrency created by FairCoop.

Recognizing a host of converging trends, many of which have been discussed in this chapter, such as the extractive approach to platform capitalism, the growing interest in people-powered platforms, and the growth in blockchain technology, a group of inspired activists and technologists have formed the Innovation Cooperative to:

> provide a space, online and off, where ideas can come together with the people, the skills, the infrastructure and the resources (including finance) to develop, hone and bring them to fruition, all within a trusted, mutually supportive environment where the platform itself is collectively owned and run by all the people that are involved.[18]

Rather than a singular focus on facilitating a cooperative model to one sector, like taxis, the Innovation Cooperative aims to use this as a platform of platforms in a way. That is to help incubate the creation of yet to be determined platform coops across a range of sectors:

> You might think of it in terms of a hackspace or fablab or even a co-working hub. It's all of these things. It's a cooperative incubator, an open cooperative development agency whose role, in part at least, is to provide everything that's needed to generate, launch and support successful cooperative platforms that can compete effectively in the market and cater to a diverse range of needs using an ethical framework that places a strong emphasis on ecological sustainability.

FUTURE OF PLATFORM COOPS

Technology can be a tool for neoliberal capitalists to try to suppress the will of the people, or it can be a democratizing force, enabling the precariat to reshape an economy that works for all. Platform coops offer an intriguing alternative to traditional capitalist models by seeking to blend the inclusive values of cooperatives with modern technology. As my colleague, Trebor Scholz recently stated, platform coops:

> can be a reminder that work can be dignified rather than diminishing for the human experience. Cooperatives are not a panacea for all the wrongs of platform capitalism but they could help to weave some ethical threads into the fabric of 21st century work.[19]

In Chapter 4, we will change directions and discuss the emergence of a range of alternative currencies and their ability to spawn new forms of PCEs, including those enabled by distributed ledger (e.g., blockchain) technologies. Besides cryptocurrencies, blockchain also enables a nascent form of PCE called distributed alternative organizations (DAOs), the subject of Chapter 5.

REFERENCES

1. Cooperative, *Wikipedia* https://en.wikipedia.org/wiki/Cooperative#cite_ref-icaprinciples_1-0. Accessed January 2017.
2. Membership in Co-operative Businesses Reaches 1 Billion, *Worldwatch Institute* http://www.worldwatch.org/membership-co-operative-businessesreaches-1-billion. Accessed January 2017.
3. http://ica.coop/sites/default/files/WCM_2016.pdf?_ga=1.33214843.495342192.1487 679260.
4. Long Island University contributor, Spanish Town Without Poverty, *News Wise*, January 2000. http://www.newswise.com/articles/view/17012. Accessed February 2017.
5. Platform.Coop book homepage, http://platform.coop/book. Accessed March 2017.
6. Peter Sims, The Real Story Behind Uber CEO, *CNN*, March 2, 2017. http://edition.cnn.com/2017/03/01/opinions/real-story-behind-uber-simsopinion/index.html. Accessed, March 2017.
7. Stocksy Homepage, About, https://www.stocksy.com/service/about/. Accessed February 2017.
8. Dan Pontefract, Platform Cooperatives Like Stocksy have a Purpose Uber and Airbnb Never Will, *Forbes*, October 2016, http://www.forbes.com/sites/danpontefract/2016/10/01/platform-cooperatives-like-stocksy-have-a-purpose uber-and-airbnb-never-will/#1772d2aa65a5. Accessed November 2016.
9. Jason Spicer, Technology Grabs Back: Platform Coops vs. the "Sharing Economy", *CoLab Radio*, December 2016. http://colabradio.mit.edu/technology-grabs-back-platform-coops-vs-the-sharing-economy/. Accessed December 2016.
10. Dobrev, Stanislav D., and Aleksios Gotsopoulos. 2010. Legitimacy vacuum, structural imprinting, and the first mover disadvantage. *Academy of Management Journal* 53(5): 1153–1174.

11. Nathan Schneider, Denver Taxi Drivers are Turning Uber's Disruption on its Head, *The Nation*, September 2016. https://www.thenation.com/article/denvertaxi-drivers-are-turning-ubers-disrup-tion-on-its-head/. Accessed November 2016.
12. Matt McFarland, Uber Blows off Regulators, Tests Self-driving Volvos in California, *CNN*, December 2016. http://money.cnn.com/2016/12/14/technology/uber-selfdriving-cars-california-dmv/index.html.
13. Fairmondo Homepage https://www.fairmondo.de/global. Accessed February 2017.
14. Wecandoit.coop Homepage http://www.wecandoit.coop. Accessed February 2017.
15. Michelle Stearn, Want to Hire a Worker-Owned-Co-op? There's an App for that Yes Magazine, April 2016. http://www.yesmagazine.org/people-power/want-to-hire-aworker-owned-co-op-theres-an-app-for-that-20160420. Accessed June 2016.
16. Daren Sharp, Why AnyShare is the First 'Complete' Cooperative in the US, *Shareable*, March 2017. http://www.shareable.net/blog/why-anyshare-is-thefirst-complete-cooperative-in-the-us. Accessed March 2017.
17. Fair.Coop Homepage https://fair.coop/faircoop/. Accessed March 2017.
18. Innovation Cooperative, *Cooperative Networks* http://networks.coop/innovation cooperative. Accessed January 2017.
19. Trebor Scholz, Platform Cooperativism vs. the Sharing Economy, *Medium*, December 2014. https://medium.com/@trebors/platform-cooperativism-vs-thesharing-economy-2ea737f1b5ad#.1rf3wok5t. Accessed September 2016.

4

Alternative Currencies and Place-Based PCE

What is money really? It is merely a mechanism for exchanging value between two or multiple parties.

Merriam Webster defines money as "something generally accepted as a medium of exchange, a measure of value, or a means of payment: such as officially coined or stamped metal currency…and paper money."[1]

Yet, this modern definition of money is biased. Before, there was paper currency backed by national and regional governments (referred to as fiat currency), gold and other metals were used to facilitate exchange. Before gold, there were many other systems like bartering whereby I made something you valued and you paid me in something I valued.

It is not very surprising that Wikipedia, a poster child of commons-based peer production, would have a more modern definition of money that better reflects a more holistic understanding of what money is or could be:

> Money is any item or verifiable record that is generally accepted as payment for goods and services and repayment of debts in a particular country or socio-economic context, or is easily converted to such a form. The main functions of money are distinguished as: a medium of exchange; a unit of account; a store of value; and, sometimes, a standard of deferred payment. Any item or verifiable record that fulfills these functions can be considered as money.[2]

We are seeing a resurgence around the globe of a range of alternative currencies from local paper currencies to digital cryptocurrencies, time banking, and gift economies. This chapter is dedicated to exploring entrepreneurship that leverages, creates, or supports such alternative currencies.*

---

* Much of this chapter was influenced by research I conducted in 2016 and published in an essay in the *Journal of Management Studies*, entitled: the Rise of Alternative Currencies in Post-capitalism.

ALTERNATIVE CURRENCIES AS A GRASSROOTS RESPONSE TO CAPITALISM

The expression that the rich keep getting richer could never be more true. Oxfam, the international nongovernment organization, has been raising awareness for the growing income inequalities around the globe for several years. In 2010, Oxfam found that the richest 388 billionaires around the globe had the same aggregate wealth that the poorest 50% of the people on the planet had (i.e., 388 people had the same wealth as about 3.5 billion people combined). That of course was pretty shocking. But maybe even more shocking is that in 2015, the number of wealthy people required to match the total income of the bottom 50% had dropped to just 62 while the top 1% of the world's wealthiest now had more combined wealth than the rest of the 99% of the world's population.[3] In 2017, the number had dwindled to just the wealthiest eight! As we continue at this pace, I suspect will soon find that one month's income of the world's richest person will equal the collective wealth of 50% of the planet (and perhaps some day 99% of the planet). An exasperated Winnie Byanyima, Director of Oxfam International, commented on the latest inequality data:

> It is obscene for so much wealth to be held in the hands of so few when 1 in 10 people survive on less than $2 a day. Inequality is trapping hundreds of millions in poverty; it is fracturing our societies and undermining democracy.
> Across the world, people are being left behind. Their wages are stagnating yet corporate bosses take home million dollar bonuses; their health and education services are cut while corporations and the super-rich dodge their taxes; their voices are ignored as governments sing to the tune of big business and a wealthy elite.[4]

What Byanyima and many in the 99% movement have been alarmed by is commonly referred to as financialization. Financialization is represented by a "pattern of accumulation in which profit making occurs increasingly through financial channels rather than through trade and commodity production."[5] Basically, financialization occurs when companies and their investors hoard their profits or place them in other financial instruments rather than put their profits back into the economy to create more value and jobs. The evidence is striking that Western economies, especially the United States, has become increasingly financialized. Between 1970 and 2010, the finance industry's percentage of the US GDP doubled, from 10% to 20%. As Forbes magazine recently summarized: "The emphasis was no longer on making things—it was making money from money."[6]

Take the case of Apple. While many debates exist regarding how much Steve Jobs' passing has affected their capability to continue to innovate, we can also observe that Apple has been sitting on massive, growing cash reserves for many years, as opposed to putting a lot of those financial windfalls back into developing many new products and services. In early 2016, Apple reportedly had $216 billion in cash and cash equivalents, although the majority of that money was placed in long-term oversees financial instruments.[7] By January 2017, Apple had accumulated 246 billion in cash reserves and securities![8]

So, financialization is helping to drive demand in alternative economic models, and a rethinking of money in society. While conducting research in the alternative currency movement, I reached out to TimeBanks.org, a US-based timebanking organization founded in 1995 to support local time banks in communities throughout the United States. I engaged in an interesting dialog with Christine Gray, the former CEO of timebanks.org who happens to have a PhD from UCLA in Political Science. In clarifying what makes timebanking, and other alternative currencies unique, Gray stated:

> The contrast with money here is instructive. Money's universality and fungability gives those who have money the ability to concentrate resources and power, and with those concentrations to channel, drive and even dominate the actions of others. Timebanking cannot concentrate wealth or power. It is in that sense a "weak" currency. That has huge implications for the way that it can be used.[*]

It must be noted that not all alternative currencies could be argued to be weak by this thinking, or at least, some may be weaker than others. For example, local paper currencies are very weak in comparison, whereas cryptocurrencies can actually be quite strong, and sometimes encourage hoarding. I will briefly expand on this in the following sections.

I believe the emergence of alternative currencies reflect a social movement, a resistance against perceived ills brought by free trade, financialization, nation building, and more recently, the increasing automation of work (i.e., industry 4.0) which is leading to a sizable increase in freelancing

---

[*] Private email correspondence with Christine Gray, of TimeBanks.org during the month of February, 2016.

and the "on-demand economy." While much of the growth in freelancing is driven by capitalist tendencies of corporations to increase efficiencies and drive down costs, as I wrote in my 2016 book about urbanpreneurs, there is also a growing interest in freelance and independent forms of work particularly among the millennial generation.

Below, I will discuss local paper currencies, cryptocurrencies, time-banking, and gift economies as primary examples of new (and historic) approaches to value exchange that also open up new, potential post-capitalist forms of entrepreneurship and small business activity.

LOCAL PAPER CURRENCIES AND HYBRID PAPER-CRYPTOCURRENCIES

In some form or another, local currencies have been around for centuries, and of course predate modern, treasury-backed currencies at the national level. But since the widespread adoption of national currencies, local alternative currencies have had a place in societies around the globe. They have been commonly implemented in a grassroots fashion as a response to economic shocks, such as in Argentina after the economic crisis around the start of the 21st century. More recently, Spain, for example, witnessed the introduction of a dozen local currencies following the 2008 crisis and, similarly, as the Wall Street Journal reported in 2015, Greece has experienced a big boost in the alternative currency movement.

According to the Complementary Currency Resource Center, there are more than 300 local paper currencies or similar currencies around the globe.[9] Perhaps surprisingly, local paper currencies are also flourishing in more than 50 communities throughout the United States.

While each local currency operates differently, these initiatives all seek to support local communities over foreign companies and investors. Local physical currencies are the epitome of weak currencies as they are virtually impossible to accumulate at any large scale that would give any single holder monopolistic rights. In fact, it would be useless to achieve such a position because local currencies are only valuable with a local, active exchange system. Therefore, I have uncovered no examples of private passive investors in local paper currencies, suggesting that this form of currency does not enable the same dispersion between corporate and investor gains without social gains. To further reduce such a risk, many local currency systems implement a negative interest rate mechanism that serves to significantly disincent their hoarding. Thus, the argument with local currency is that it has the potential to increase the velocity of local transactions and exchange of value in the community. The United Kingdom has a very active local currency movement, and researchers recently determined that local spending with local currencies leads to a 4× increase in value to the neighborhood as the money continues to circulate locally.[10]

Entrepreneurship and Small Business Associated with Local Currencies

BerkShares, founded in 2006 in Berkshire, Massachusetts, are acquired by exchanging US dollars for this local currency, which then must remain in the community. More than 400 local businesses in the community accept BerkShares for payment. The goal of BerkShares is to "maximize the circulation of goods, services, and capital within the region... and to distinguish the local businesses that accept the currency from those that do not." Clearly, small, local businesses have been willing to engage in local paper currency exchange. This could not work easily for businesses that are dependent on acquiring products from international suppliers since the revenues generated locally from the paper currency may not be easily exchanged in international markets. Note, some local currency programs have mechanisms for small businesses to exchange their local currencies received to a national currency for a fee when it is necessary to obtain supplies outside of the community.

Perhaps, the largest currently operating local currency is in Bristol, UK. Currently, more than 700 local small businesses in Bristol accept payment via the local Bristol Pound. I would list the types of services one can pay for with a Bristol Pound but that would take quite a few pages. There are more than 120 types of local service providers who accept the pound. You could live your whole life in Bristol and virtually not want for anything relying only on exchanging local currency. You can have a timber home designed by architects from Askew Cavanna; you can buy your food at a local coop, baker, or butcher; get your hair cut at Sarah's Barbering, have your child cared for at The Bubbahub, do your banking at the Bristol Credit Union, pay your energy bill from Bristol Energy or cocreate and consume with Bristol Energy Co-operative, have all your wedding needs arranged from Absolutely Cakes, Ido Wedding Films, and Nicki Breeze Photography and of course get your hands on some local, handcrafted artisanal beer from the Bristol Beer Factory. The City Council of Bristol, recognizing the challenges of some small businesses in having to obtain fiat currency, permits participating Bristol Pound businesses to pay local business and individual taxes with the Bristol Pound.

The Bristol Pound is one of a number of local currency systems that have shifted to a hybrid model with both physical notes and electronic payments accepted at participating retailers. The technology is allowing local retailers to also attract younger customers who embrace the values of the local currency movement and appreciate the convenience of making purchases with their smart phone directly.

A local restaurant owner in Liverpool where they also recently introduced their own local Pound, noted:

> We're already getting new customers coming in wanting to pay with new currency partly out of curiosity as well as a belief it's the right thing to do. It's a great conversation starter because when you pay, you see each other's name and picture on your device, so you're already building a relationship. From the chats we're having, it seems people understand you can't moan about your high street being packed with charity shops unless you do something about it and support local, independent businesses.[11]

Of course, local currencies are not only about supporting local, small businesses but also about enabling local residents to appreciate their role in improving their local communities through the purchases they make. The implementation of local currencies, especially when coupled with hybrid mobile payment options, can also inspire new startup activity as well. Colu is a startup founded in Tel Aviv at the end of 2014 dedicated to enabling cities create their own local, digital currency through a mobile application leveraging blockchain technology.

> We believe that real change begins at the local level. Through the use of local currencies, more people shop local, eat local, buy local, and live local, strengthening the local economy, and keeping the control of money in everyone's hands. With a strong and inclusive local economy people feel more connected to one another, increasing social responsibility and social capital.

At the risk of sounding like a hypocrite, I would like to draw your attention to the fact that Colu has raised more than $12 million in venture capital investment since its founding. While later in this book, I will talk about how venture capital is dead in a post-capitalist society, there are companies who may support our transition to post-capitalism who may very well receive venture capital to scale their solutions. Colu is one such company. Colu is behind the launch of the Liverpool Pound's mobile platform after having launched Colu in two cities in Israel. In Liverpool, Colu's revenue model is based on charging local retailers £25 per month for participation in the Liverpool Pound program. Additionally, in hopes of deterring Liverpool Pound users from taking the local currency out of circulation via exchanging or UK pounds, Colu charges 5% of the amount being removed from the user's digital wallet.

I had the opportunity to speak with Colu's CEO and cofounder Amos Meiri, who believes the firm's for-profit venture backing improves the ability for digital local currencies to succeed:

> The reason they never picked up and became something big is because they were managed by non-profit volunteers, but we are a very ambitious start-up with investors behind us.[12]

This is an interesting perspective as many people in the PCE world do not believe that trying to scale singular venture-capital-backed enterprises will help transition us to this new future economy. Yet, throughout this book, I will share examples of startups, some of which have or may attain venture capital and may also play a role in a successful transition to PCE. Colu's mobile technology, backed by blockchain, which I will discuss at great length in Chapter 5, is something that could be difficult for local organizations and cities to develop and continually support over time. If digital local currencies are going to be important in a PCE economy, than Colu and other startups like them could be of great use in streamlining community's efforts to embrace such currency. At the same time, it is clear that the partnership between the private sector and local communities in enabling such solutions could pose risks since the private provider may deviate from the values of the community in an effort to maximize profits. For these hybrid organizations that help the transition toward PCE, it would be useful if, for example, they committed to becoming B Corps or something similar as it could mitigate the risk they end up similar to Uber!

BORDERLESS CRYPTOCURRENCIES

The growing hybrid approaches to local paper and digital currencies provide a nice transition to discuss the rampant growth of cryptocurrencies around the globe. The first-known experiments with cryptocurrencies occurred in the Netherlands in the mid-1980s. Yet, cryptocurrencies took off as something of note with the introduction of Bitcoin in 2008. The brainchild of a mysterious and as of yet unidentified person or group of persons, with the pseudonym, Satashio Nakamoto, Bitcoin emerged as a global, digital currency not controlled or supported by any government, that is, a borderless, digital, alternative currency. Bitcoin is intended to be an anonymous digital currency that allows for transactions between individuals without intermediaries. If I own bitcoins and want to buy your computer with bitcoins, we can agree on the value of the computer and I can transfer the Bitcoin equivalent value to you immediately.

Cryptocurrencies such as Bitcoin are not really weak currencies as it is possible for an individual or group of individuals to accumulate bitcoins or even engage in currency speculation. The Bitcoin protocol has established that there will never be more than 21 million total bitcoins in circulation. The fact that there is a maximum limit could eventually incent investors and speculators to hoard bitcoins in the hopes that hoarding bitcoins could lead to a shortage and drive up their value.

Bitcoin is far from the only cryptocurrency gaining steam globally. Coinmarketcorp.com is a leading website tracking the cryptocurrency marketplace. At the time of writing, they were tracking nearly 650 different cryptocurrencies. The market capitalization for the top 100 such currencies, as of February 2017 was reported to be almost $20 billion and as of June 2017, the total market capitalization for all cryptocurrencies surpassed 100 billion (USD)! (https://www.cryptocoinsnews.com/digital-currencies-market-cap-breaches-100-billion/). Table 4.1 summarizes the top 10 most valued cryptocurrencies in the world, with Bitcoin of course leading the list along with their per unit price, supply, and 24-hour trading volume on February 6, 2017.

CRYPTOCURRENCY STARTUPS

Cryptocurrencies may appear to be out of context in a book about post-capitalist entrepreneurship. In fact, Bitcoin has had some big successes in the startup community with more than US$1.35 billion venture capital invested in Bitcoin startups since 2012 and $890 million in 2015 alone.[13] Venture-backed cryptocurrency startups have emerged in dozens of sectors,

TABLE 4.1

Largest Cryptocurrencies by Market Capitalization

Currency	Market Cap ($)	Price ($)	Available Supply	Volume (24 hour) ($)
Bitcoin	16,746,889,911	1,037.09	16,147,962 BTC	114,724,000
DigiCube	1,057,507,938	0.52	2,018,402,999 CUBE	677
Ethereum	1,014,080,978	11.44	88,620,977 ETH	6,084,130
Ripple	236,349,395	0.01	36,856,513,336 XRP	313,435
Litecoin	200,936,383	4.05	49,670,706 LTC	5,043,420
Monero	177,408,034	12.77	13,895,610 XMR	2,136,960
Ethereum Classic	131,856,420	1.49	88,581,039 ETC	2,584,770
Dash	120,352,000	16.99	7,082,988 DASH	1,193,310
NEM	53,142,030	0.01	8,999,999,999 XEM	382,903
Steem	37,509,590	0.16	232,158,333 STEEM	71,951

Source: Coinmarketcorp.com

including hardware, software, mobile payments, financial services, and commerce, all obvious opportunities for helping to establish the cryptocurrency infrastructure. But other startups have explored the growing infrastructure to offer services in niche areas, such as tourism. BTC Trip, for example, was established as a travel agency for Bitcoin users, allowing them to book travel with Bitcoin instead of fiat currency. In 2013 and 2014, BTC Trip raised $175,000 in seed capital from angel investors. Unfortunately, it appears BC Trip did not survive beyond the end of 2016. Of course, the startup world is always risky, probably more so, in these bleeding-edge spaces that are merging the world of technology and post-capitalism.

> It's important to remember we are at the very start of this industry and being too early can be dangerous. I therefore focus on companies that have the potential to scale their revenues (and ultimately profits) in a reasonable amount of time despite the industry's relative immaturity. In many cases, one invests in a company that already operates in a large market; in the Bitcoin space it is different—it is a fast growing but small market; the key is therefore to identify companies that can scale quickly in spite of the initial small size of the market.[14] (Pamir Gelenbe, Partner Hummingbird Ventures)

Still there are many firms that have gained a lot of traction in the cryptocurrency arena although many of these players and their investors are primarily focused on building very scalable, and profitable, startups in the market economy. However, Bitcoin and other cryptocurrencies emerged as part of the 99% movement and the frustration with banks too big to fail and the failure of federal governments to implement policies which yield prosperity for all income classes. It is possible that Bitcoin may end up being just another form of market-based capitalism. I hold out hope that we will see a growing number of PCEs emerge in this space as well.

CRYPTOCURRENCIES AND PCE

So up until now, this section on cryptocurrencies has probably left most of the passionate post-capitalist readers disappointed. All this talk of scalable venture-capital-backed Bitcoin startups seems a long way from the PCE I have described throughout much of this book. Let's look at organizations embracing PCE and cryptocurrencies more directly. But first, an introduction to initial coin offerings (ICOs).

INITIAL COIN OFFERINGS

Cryptocurrency startups aim to create digital currencies not regulated by national or regional governments. As you will see later, many such initiatives have goals highly aligned with the PCE movement documented throughout this book. But you may be wondering how do cryptocurrencies get off the ground. Through what is referred to as an ICO. An ICO is a lot like crowdfunding in that what it does is aim to generate capital for the launch of the project from a distributed audience of interested stakeholders. ICOs are commonly referred to as crowdsales because rather than raising money as equity investment in a startup, ICOs are used by cryptocurrency startups as a way to fund, and put a value on, a new digital currency. One of the most successful ICOs to date was that of Ethereum, considered by some to be more stable and promising than Bitcoin. To get Ethereum off the ground, the founders, in 2014, initiated an ICO raising $18 million worth of Bitcoin (i.e., the early "investors" in Ethereum used Bitcoin to purchase Ether tokens). At the time of the offering, the value of Ether tokens was 40 cents. As can be seen from the Table 4.1, Ether tokens have done very well, rising to more than $11 (USD), in early 2017 before surpassing $260 (USD) and a market capitalization of more than 24 billion (USD) by June 2017.

In March 2017, I met Richard Kastelein, the founder of Blockchain News, who has been involved in several ICOs. I followed up with him later to get his insights on where ICOs are and where they are going. He shared with me a working paper he has been writing on the topic of ICOs. Here are a few interesting passages:

> Imagine open sourcing all your software and structuring the company as a non-profit foundation bypassing the VC route, designing your own currency and assigning a value to it and selling it... raising millions—and imagine doing all this without having even built any software and just putting an idea down on paper—essentially offering vapourware with a bit of math and text on a few pages called a "whitepaper"...
>
> Welcome to the new world of Initial Coin Offerings (ICOs)—a phenomenon born from the Bitcoin community that is rocking the venture capital industry, who are now beginning to take a good, hard look at this new financial instrument which has both its benefits and its disadvantages as well as threats and opportunities to their own business model.[15]

While ICOs are starting to attract venture capital investment and traditional market enterprises, they are also opening up interesting financing options for those interested in embracing the commons and PCE.

> For Blockchain startups it's a win-win—there's no equity stakeholders breathing down their necks and many feel there's finally a solution for non-profit foundations who want to build open-source software to find capital. As they hold a percentage of the total cryptocurrency in circulation (usually 10–20 percent) they also have a vested interest in building more value.[16]

Below I will highlight a few interesting cryptocurrencies, many of which have launched with ICOs who do reflect the values of PCE.

FairCoin

FairCoin is one of the most ambitious cryptocurrencies with respect to goals of supporting a transition to post-capitalism. FairCoin is a blockchain-enabled initiative of FairCoop, mentioned in Chapter 3 as a pioneering platform of platforms. Consistent with the transformative mission of FairCoop, FairCoin aims to "be used as a tool for economic redistribution, increasing justice, the empowerment of grassroots groups, the transformation of social and economic relations and the creation of commons."[17]

The FairCoin creators from FairCoop have built in mechanisms into the cryptocurrency to try to ensure more equitable access to FairCoin while also minimizing the energy consumed to maintain and mine FairCoin compared with other digital currencies.* FairCoin does not have the traction of the other major cryptocurrencies at the moment but it has certainly garnered the attention of those interested in the PCE angle of cryptocurrency. At the time of writing, one FairCoin was equivalent to 11 cents, yielding a market capitalization of 5.8 million (USD).

SolarCoin

SolarCoin was founded in January, 2014, by Nick Gogerty and Joseph Zitoli. The SolarCoin Foundation aims to be a digital currency that "works like air miles for solar electricity generation."[18] For people, like homeowners, who invest in generating their own solar energy, they can apply online to obtain solar coins. For each megawatt of solar energy generated, the producer receives one virtual solar coin for free. The SolarCoin Foundation embraces transparency through the blockchain and relies on a global network of volunteers who support the growth of the SolarCoin community. Solar coins can be converted to bitcoins and then used for transactions on Bitcoin platforms or even later swapped for global currencies. In early 2017, SolarCoin had a market capitalization of more than US$11 million and each coin was being traded at 11.2 cents.[19]

By August, 2016, $34 million worth of solar coins were in circulation. The overall program designed by the Solar Coin Foundation was designed to last 40 years with a plan to eventually deliver nearly 100 billion solar coins reflecting nearly 100,000 TerraWatts hours of solar electricity.[20]

HealthCoin

Nick Gogerty is at it again. Just 2 years after cofounding SolarCoin, he cofounded HealthCoin with a similar approach to using alternative

---

* While this is outside the scope of this chapter, it is worth mentioning that cryptocurrency "mining" and maintenance can be extremely energy intensive. Several studies have measured the growing energy requirements for the execution of just one single transaction of Bitcoin, for example. Some experts even predict that the Bitcoin ecosystem will consume as much energy as the entire nation of Denmark by just 2020.

currencies as incentives for a more social and sustainable society. In this case, HealthCoin encourages users to:

> input biomarkers. Healthcoins are generated when users change or maintain biomarkers indicating diabetes prevention. Users own their health information and choose who to share it to, and a dashboard helps them track and understand their health.

HealthCoins are then issued as incentives to users as they meet and exceed recommended guidelines for diabetes prevention. Each user may have their own "prevention network" such as employers, health care providers, or nonprofit groups who can create their own exchange system for HealthCoins.

Bitcoin for the Unbanked

Approximately 2.5 billion adults around the world have no access to a banking account. Along with their dependent children, approximately 5 billion people in the world are unbanked. Blockchain and other cryptocurrencies are seen as a potential solution to this massive problem. In Africa, where as many as 80% of adults are unbanked, several startups have emerged exploring how cryptocurrencies can improve access to participating in transactions previously out of reach for many. For example, Azteco has signed up thousands of small convenience stores to become a type of ATM service for the unbanked. A local, unbanked resident of Lagos, Nigeria, for example, can go to a local merchant and present cash to the staff who then create vouchers redeemable in Bitcoin equivalents. The resident can then convert these vouchers online for use with e-commerce applications or other local and global remittances where cash is not possible (or unreasonable expensive via services like Western Union).

TIMEBANKING

In 1832, a Welsh socialist launched one of the first-known timebanks, called the National Equitable Labour Exchange. Since then, timebanking has remained a fringe, low-tech, and highly localized mechanism to encourage local community members to contribute their expertise to their neighbors in return for an equivalent amount of time from someone else in the community. The recipient of the original service is not obligated to deliver a service in return to the same member, but, instead, becomes indebted to the community and will owe an equivalent amount of time to another member. It is virtually impossible to accumulate time credit to a point where any individual in the community can exert monopoly power over the community. Thus, timebanking is clearly a weak currency.

Historically, timebanking has been a very localized phenomenon relying on locally provided services to other members living in close proximity. In the late 20th century, basic software programs and the Internet itself became tools for local timebanking services to improve the efficiency of the service. Even today, several timebanking and software organizations are committed to open-source software tools to allow local organizers to quickly launch their own timebanks. Community Weaver was developed as an open-source software tool for local timebanks by Timebanks USA. Time and Talents is another open-source timebanking solution made available by hOurworld, an international timebanking network, to any community group interested in starting their own local timebanking initiative. hOurworld currently has more than 40,000 members in 660 communities around the world with more than 2 million hours exchanged.

Yet, new social networking and video technologies allow for timebanking to potentially scale regionally or even globally. Brazil-based Bliive, for example, has facilitated the sharing of more than 100,000 hours of expertise in return for time credit through an online platform which connects primarily local timebankers to exchange value and expertise. Although in the case of Bliiive, their technology still primarily facilitates local interactions, I believe we are on the cusp of seeing more global forms of timebanking, whereby professionals across a range of disciplines could offer their expertise for primarily short interactions with those seeking their expertise around the globe. Why couldn't a doctor in Germany seeing her first case of the Zika virus use a timebanking platform to solicit expertise from a Brazilian doctor who has treated hundreds of cases? Or an aspiring electric vehicle carsharing entrepreneur in Seoul obtain insights from a city administrator supporting Autolib in Paris leveraging a global timebanking platform?

Time Republik founded in 2012 by Gabriele Donati and Karim Varini in Lugano, Switzerland, is getting closer to that vision. Today, they have representation in the United States, Italy, Switzerland, Brazil, Spain, France, Germany, Denmark, Russia, and the Netherlands. Time Republik claims to have timebankers in more than 100 countries sharing 100,000 talents.

Their model requires that all hours are created equal, that is, regardless of your expertise, 1 hour offered to members is equal to 1 hour of any other expertise offered on the platform. This works well for most locally delivered services, but it could explain why they do not have many highly educated professionals delivering global expertise and instead still primarily rely on members exchanging expertise locally. One revenue model of note for Time Republik is that they offer their software, not for free as open source, but rather for a monthly fee as a white label to companies, nonprofits, and governments interested in facilitating timebanking within their communities. However, Time Republik does not monetize the timesharing activities of its members. Furthermore, Time Republik even allows users to choose to gift their time instead of banking it. This leads to the last form of alternative currency I wish to highlight in this chapter, the gift economy.

GIFT ECONOMY

I must admit the first time I heard the term gift economy, I thought it was a bit silly. I thought it was about people giving either paid for, or self-made, gifts to their friends and family. Thankfully, it is much bigger than that. The gift economy is about gifting items or services usually to strangers generally without expectation of receiving any item or monetary compensation in return. Of course, the gift economy existed well before currencies were invented and often coincided with bartering where some products or services could be exchanged for other products and services. My colleagues Duncan McLaren and Julian Agyeman, authors of the book *Sharing Cities*, refer to the gift economy as karmic altruism because in many cases individuals believe that somehow, indirectly karma will be nice to them.

What actually constitutes the gift economy is still disputed. There are many gray areas in the overlap between the gift economy, peer-to-peer sharing economy, cooperatives, bartering, and other alternative models of value creation and exchange. ServiceSpace, originally founded in 1999, focuses on promoting what they refer to as generosity-driven projects around the world. They have done more thinking than most about what are the key elements of the gift economy and what types of gift economies are in operation around the globe. With respect to key aspects of the gift economy, ServiceSpace suggests that for something to be part of a gift economy, it should ideally meet the following criteria: (1) there is an act of selflessness on the part of the giver; (2) the giver is not expected to place any value on the gift, but instead the receiver is in the role of placing a value on it, not in a monetary sense; and (3) ideally, it is not seen as a one-off gift but a gift that keeps on giving by reinforcing a true gift economy through facilitating a virtuous circle of giving within the community.

Furthermore, ServiceSpace highlights a handful of types of activities within the gift economy including[21]:

- Charitable donations—philanthropic gifts of money, goods, or services
- Donation requested—donation requested adds some element of compelling individuals to donate[22]:

> I think of Wikipedia's frequent postings on their page to encourage donations. Wikipedia is one of the most visited websites in the world. Commerce is fine. Advertising is not evil. But it doesn't belong here. Not in Wikipedia. Wikipedia is something special. It is like a library or a public park. It is like a temple for the mind. It is a place we can all go to think, to learn, to share our knowledge with others. When I founded Wikipedia, I could have made it into a for-profit company with advertising banners, but I decided to do something different. We've worked hard over the years to keep it lean and tight. We fulfill our mission efficiently. If everyone reading this donated, our fundraiser would be done within an hour. But not everyone can or will donate. And that's fine. Each year just enough people decide to give. This year, please consider making a donation of $5, $20, $50 or whatever you can to protect and sustain Wikipedia. Jimmy Wales (Wikipedia Founder)

- *Portion of proceeds donated*—when a company agrees to allocate a percentage of revenues or profits to social or environmental causes. One per cent for the Planet, for example, an initiative founded by the forward-thinking clothing retailer, Patagonia, commits member companies to donate 1% of revenues to environmental causes. Over 1,300 startups, companies, and nonprofits around the globe have committed to 1% for the Planet.
- *Proceeds of sale donated*—speaking of Patagonia, during the 2016 Black Friday sales, Patagonia agreed to dedicate 100% of their revenues from that day to local environmental groups.[23] The interesting thing about this model is that there is a cash transaction between the

seller and buyer but 100% of the revenue (not just profits) is gifted to charity. Late! was founded in 2008 in Chile by Pedro Traverso who had recently completed his Master's in engineering from the University of California, Berkeley. Travesero connected with four other like-minded founders to create a company whose goal was entirely to give back to society by committing to gifting 100% of their profits to foundations serving the most vulnerable of Chile. Late! primarily sells bottled water, harnessed and packaged in more sustainable ways than most of the industry, through traditional retailers. To date, Late! has donated about 200 million Chilean pesos (more than US$300,000) to Chilean foundations. Late! further etched its commitment to being a social enterprise when it became B Corp certified in 2012.

- *Pay as you will*—Here the idea is that the provider offers the service and the user pays what they feel the service is worth, what they can afford, or perhaps even pay more to gift future lower-income customers. Karma Kitchen first opened in Berkeley in 2007, "by several volunteers inspired to seed the value of a gift economy."[24] Today, Karma Kitchen has more than 20 restaurants in 10 countries where consumers receive no official bill, but the eaters can choose to pay nothing or as much as they'd like.

- *Pay it forward*—Karma Kitchen itself could be a pay it forward model. Pay it forward is the idea where you may receive something free and then contribute what you want for future eaters.

- *Collectivism*—When collective groups of individuals in society pool resources and skills together to share widely without regard to how much each person is contributing to the collective. ColletiveOne is an interesting example of a PCE organization that is based broadly on the concept of collectivism and alternative currency. CollectiveOne was found by a group of individuals committed to the commons and open collaboration. In fact, the CollectiveOne platform itself was developed in the same way that the platform now allows others to create collective projects together. CollectiveOne serves as an open software tool (licensed under Creative Commons) that allows anyone to start the creation of some kind of project and to reach agreement with others who have skills that can advance the project along. The original creator can offer points (a type of alternative currency in CollectiveOne) for each contribution made along the way. CollectiveOne therefore tries to create a type of virtual collective with each member contributing what they are able to. Colony.io is a similar initiative but for-profit and leveraging blockchain technology.

- http://www.glasgowcollective.com
- *Cooperativism*—The idea behind cooperatives, which have existed for centuries, is that individuals can collaborate in the ownership and governance of an organization which can be for-profit or non-profit with the goal of sharing resources, expertise, or income within the cooperative. While cooperatives often operate within capitalist markets, I consider them to be part of a transition to a post-capitalist society. In this book, there is a whole chapter dedicated to platform cooperatives (Chapter 3).

There are many intriguing examples of people and organizations pushing the limits of what we consider to be entrepreneurial activity as part of this broader framing of the gift economy. Below, I will highlight just a few of my favorites along with some words of caution for aspiring gift economy entrepreneurs.

Repair Cafes

In 2007, frustrated with the amount of waste in society, Martine Postma conceived of the idea of a Repair Café, whereby, once a month, people in Amsterdam who were good at fixing things could be matched with people who had broken household items. The idea was to bring the community together but to prohibit monetary exchanges. Instead, the Repair Café builds community while keeping more products from going to the landfill. Postma had no economic motivation for starting the first Repair Café. Today, committed to the commons, she led the creation of the Repair Café International Foundation to allow organizers around the world to start their own Repair Cafes. Today, there are more than 1,200 active Repair Cafes, with 1,000 in Europe alone!

Peerby

Peerby was founded in 2011 and perhaps not coincidentally also got their start in Amsterdam. Peerby by the way is now a certified B Corp, which was the subject of Chapter 2. Amsterdam has established itself as a leader in Europe in the promotion of the sharing economy. Peerby started exclusively as a platform to facilitate households to share household items with their neighbors.

Today, Peerby encourages sharing of items for home improvement, moving, hosting parties, vacation supplies (e.g., tents, suitcases), and garden equipment. Peerby claims to have more than $1 billion worth of items freely available for borrowing in more than 20 European cities plus the United States. While their original model is clearly part of the gift economy in the sense that there was no expectation of monetary compensation for lending these items, Peerby has since evolved to also offer paid rental service, Peerby Go, for curated catalogue of products with guaranteed availability, delivery, and insurance. Therefore, Peerby runs the free lending platform concurrently with the new paid rental service, although this service is primarily focused on the United States and the United Kingdom. In order to finance the growth of Peerby, they launched a crowdfunding campaign on OnePlanetCrowd.com and were able to raise $2.2 million in just one weekend from more than 1,000 individuals, mostly Dutch users of the free Peerby platform. This campaign made the "crowd the largest shareholder" of Peerby!

TOMS Shoes: A Great Story and a Note of Caution!

By now, many readers have probably heard of TOMS Shoes. It has widely been viewed as a success story and a pioneer in new models for the gift economy. The inspiration for TOMS Shoes has been told thousands of times. But to summarize, Blake Mycoskie was traveling in Argentina in 2006 and noticed how many impoverished children were walking around without shoes. Recognizing shoes as a basic need that could prevent illness and injury, he conceived of the idea of a shoe company that charged a little more for a pair of shoes in order to finance the donation of another pair of shoes for children in developing countries. So, a purchaser of TOMS Shoes in say the United States could feel good about their shoes knowing that they also were responsible for the gift of shoes to a shoeless child. TOMS claims to have gifted more than 50 million shoes since the company was started. In 2014, a private equity firm, Bain Capital acquired 50% of TOMS Shoes, valuing the company at more than US$600 million.[25] Impressive right?

While the buy one, gift one model has been embraced in other sectors as well, TOMS has been the subject of much criticism. Particularly, critics note that giving shoes does not actually solve many problems in poor communities, and in fact, can actually hurt the local economy where there are local artisans and crafts people who try to make a living producing and selling low-cost local shoes in these communities. And because TOMS has been producing the shoes in the United States and China, there is no sustainable impact on local economies. William Easterly, an Economics Professor at NYU, stated that "TOMS shoes Buy 1 Give 1 keeps surpassing its record as worst charity in development."[26]

Unlike many successful founders, however, Mycoskie has recognized the flaws in his business model raised by critics. In recent years, TOMS has begun producing shoes in developing countries that are also recipients of the gifted shoes such as Ethiopia, Kenya, and Haiti among others with a goal of having 30% of all shoe production in recipient countries.

Online Giving

In the past decade, we have seen several new models of online giving. Here, I will highlight two such models that have focused on giving between residents in the developed world and those in the developing world.

Kiva is "a non-profit organization with a mission to connect people through lending to alleviate poverty. Leveraging the internet and a worldwide network of microfinance institutions, Kiva lets individuals lend as little as $25 to help create opportunity around the world." I consider Kiva part of the gift economy because Kiva and its network do not offer interest on the loans provided by people like you and I. It is kind of like a gift that keeps on giving because the loans are offered to microentrepreneurs in the developing world. When the loans are paid off, the lender can choose to keep the money in the Kiva system lending to other microentrepreneurs. Kiva claims to have a 97.1% repayment rate across the 82 countries where it works and has served more than 1.5 million individuals.

GiveDirectly is an impressive gift economy PCE. It was originally founded in 2009 as a private giving circle by four Harvard and MIT students who were convinced that there could be better and more direct ways of giving to people in low-income countries. GiveDirectly, a registered nonprofit, has exploded since opening to the public in 2011 and has now facilitated $100 million in direct giving between people in high-income countries to Kenya and Uganda. GiveDirectly considers its model to be part of an unconditional basic income to its recipients. Perhaps not surprisingly given the founders educational backgrounds, GiveDirectly is committed to supporting academic research to improve efficiency of the donations on its platform. Research from Innovations for Poverty Action studied the use of the donations by recipients in Kenya and found:

> Increases in expenditure across all categories measured, including food, medical and education expenses, durables, home improvement, and social events. It also found large increases in income and in asset holdings, in particular livestock, furniture, and iron roofs.

GiveDirectly is clearly a different model than Kiva. Kiva relies on a network of local microfinance institutions, treats gifts as loans, and also charges high interest rates to the recipients. The funding is conditional in the sense that it is designed to support a microenterprise and the loan must be repaid back with interest payments covering the operating expenses of the microfinance institutions. GiveDirectly on the other hand offers unconditional basic income payments directly to the poorest in their target countries with no intermediaries, allowing them to have the highest efficiency of any donation model.

CONCLUSION

If we are to challenge the assumption that capitalism is the best economic model for delivering equitable, inclusive well-being, it is imperative we challenge the role of the underlying monetary supply, and furthermore, our perception of how value is created and exchanged in society. This chapter was dedicated to exploring alternative currencies and their potential role in a transition to a post-capitalist society through PCE. Much of the chapter was focused on the explosion of alternative currencies, most of which are backed by blockchain. Blockchain and other distributed ledger technologies are at the core of an emerging movement to develop decentralized autonomous organizations, which are the subject of Chapter 5.

REFERENCES

1. Merriam Webster Dictionary, https://www.merriam-webster.com/dictionary/money. Accessed February 2017.
2. Money, Wikipedia, https://en.wikipedia.org/wiki/Money. Accessed February 6, 2017.

3. John Slater, 62 People Own the Same as Half the World, reveals Oxfam Davos Report, *Oxfam,* January 2016 https://www.oxfam.org/en/pressroom/pressreleases/2016-01-18/62-people-own-same-half-world-reveals-oxfam-davosreport. Accessed February 2017.

4. Anna Ratcliff, Just 8 Men Own Same Wealth as Half the World, *Oxfam,* January 2017. https://www.oxfam.org/en/pressroom/pressreleases/2017-01-16/just-8-men-own-same-wealth-half-world. Accessed February 2017.

5. Krippner, G. R. 2005. The financialization of the American economy. *Socio-Economic Review* 3: 173–208.

6. Mike Collins, Wall Street and the Financialization of the Economy, *Forbes,* February 2015. http://www.forbes.com/sites/mikecollins/2015/02/04/wallstreet-and- the- financialization-of-the-economy/#17bfc5de2c1b. Accessed January 2017.

7. Jeremy Owens, Apple Really isn't Sitting on $216 billion in Cash, *Market Watch,* January 2016. http://www.marketwatch.com/story/apple-isnt-really-sittingon-216-billion-in-cash-2016-01-26. Accessed January 2017.

8. Christine Wang, Apple's Cash Hoard Swells to Record $246.09 billion, *CNBC,* January 2017. http://www.cnbc.com/2017/01/31/apples-cash-hoard-swells-torecord-24609- billion.html. Accessed January 2017.

9. Complentary Currency http://www.complementarycurrency.org/ccDatabase/. Accessed October 2016.

10. Sean Hargrave, Love your Local? Liverpool Joins Cohort of Community Currencies, *The Guardian,* February 2017, https://www.theguardian.com/small-business-network/2017/feb/03/love-localliverpool-joins-cohort-community-currencies. Accessed February 2017.

11. Sean Hargrave, Love your Local? Liverpool Joins Cohort of Community Currencies, The Guardian, February 2017, https://www.theguardian.com/small-business network/2017/feb/03/love-local-liverpool-joins-cohort-community-currencies. Accessed February 2017.

12. Rebecca Campbell, Liverpool Gets its Own Digital Currency, *Cryptocoins News,* February 2017. https://www.cryptocoinsnews.com/liverpool-gets-digital-currency/. Accessed February 2017.

13. Blockchain Venture Capital *Coindesk* http://www.coindesk.com/bitcoin-venture capital/. Accessed February 6, 2017.

14. Jonathon Chester, What Venture Capitalists Look for in a Blockchain Startup, *Forbes,* June 2016. http://www.forbes.com/sites/jonathanchester/2016/06/16/what-venture- capitalists- look-for-in-ablockchain-startup/#91d1d634c2dc. Accessed February 2017.

15. R. Kastelein, *Working Paper Entitled: Tokenization in the Age of Blockchain,* 2017.

16. Fair.Coin Homepage, https://fair.coop/faircoin/. Accessed March 2017.

17. Solar Coin FAQ, https://solarcoin.org/en/faq-frequently-asked-questions/. Accessed March 2017.

18. Crypto Currency Market Capitalizations, *Coin Market Cap,* http://coinmarketcap.com/currencies/views/market-cap-by-total-supply/. Accessed January 2017.

19. Michael Scott, Asset Profile: SolarCoin, *Coincap News* August 2016. http://news.coincap.io/2016/08/featured-asset-profile-solarcoin/. Accessed March 2017.

20. Defining Gift Economy, *Service Space* https://www.servicespace.org/join/?pg=gift. Accessed November 2016.

21. Jimmy Wales, Ways to Give, Wikimedia, https://donate.wikimedia.org/w/index. php?title=Special:FundraiserLandingPage&country=XX&uselang=en&utm_ medium=sidebar&utm_source=donate&utm_ campaign=C13_en.wikipedia.org. Accessed November 2016.

22. Rose Marcario, 100 Percent Today, 1 Percent Every Day, *Patagonia,* November 2016. http://www.patagonia.com/blog/2016/11/100-percent-today-1-percent-every-day/. Accessed March 2017.

23. Karma Kitchen Home http://www.karmakitchen.org/index.php?pg=about. Accessed November 2016.

24. Greg Roumeliotis and Olivia Oran, *Bain Capital to Invest in Shoemaker Toms,* August 2014. http://www.reuters.com/article/us-toms-baincapitalidUSKBN0GK 1ZZ20140820. Accessed November 2016.

25. William Easterly, *Twitter,* April 2012. https://twitter.com/bill_easterly/ status/186826099743924227. Accessed November 2016.

26. J. Haushofer and J. Shapiro, 2013. Household Response to Income Changes: Evidence from Unconditional Cash Transfer Program in Kenya, Massachusetts Institute of Technology, Boston. http://www.princeton.edu/~joha/publications/ Haushofer_Shapiro_UCT_2013.pdf. Accessed March 2017.

5

The Distributed Autonomous Organization

The previous chapters have focused on emergent organizational forms that have significant traction around the world and are already clearly demonstrating the potential for a more democratized economy as groups of individuals form alternatives to capitalist models of organizing the economy. We have seen a range from transitionary capitalist models, like B Corps and platform cooperatives, to more post-capitalist models like commons-based peer production and models based on alternative currencies. In all of those chapters, there are organizations that have existed for a few years or more, that have growing user bases and buy-in from virtual or physical communities. This chapter is about a bleeding-edge organizational model, that to me, probably represents the most post-capitalist technologically-enabled organizing model, distributed autonomous organizations (DAOs).

Beyond platform cooperatives, which still technically operate within capitalist models, there is a new PCE model called a distributed autonomous organization which has only emerged in the past few years. In this chapter, I will highlight a handful of emerging DAOs that show the potential (and pitfalls) of DAOs, while keeping an eye toward the future impact DAOs could have on society and our economy, and "business" models we are yet to see but probably will soon.

A DAO is basically a mashup between open-source software (Chapter 1) and platform cooperatives (Chapter 3). A DAO is technically not even an enterprise, but rather based on software developed and enhanced through the community. But rather than say Wikipedia which is an open-source tool for sharing knowledge, DAOs are open-source tools for facilitating exchanges between peers and other organizations. Remember the discussion in Chapter 3 about the Denver taxi drivers who decided to fight Uber with a platform cooperative model? While a platform cooperative, by its nature, is owned by its members, a DAO is owned by no one. Instead, it is a project that enables transactions without any intermediary ownership at all.

This is not science fiction either. Backed primarily by distributed ledger technologies (DLTs) like blockchain and ethereum which were initially conceived to support the digital currencies discussed in Chapter 4, DAOs are emerging as we speak, or perhaps as I write. Can DAOs operate locally, leveraging distributed global tech to support local ecosystems and P2P interaction? How will conflicts be resolved? Is it really possible to have a P2P platform with no intermediary? Will there be any revenue models that emerge for the collaborative group who develops and maintains the DAO platform? In this chapter, I seek to answer, or at least shed light on, some of these questions while providing some insights on emerging examples of DAOs. First, a brief summary of DLT as this serves as the foundation for DAOs.

DISTRIBUTED LEDGER TECHNOLOGY

All the early attention about Bitcoin regarded its potential disruptive capability for our global monetary supply. Many thought Bitcoin would disintermediate banks and be one of the biggest technological innovations of our generation. Venture capitalists began pouring money into Bitcoin startups to the tune of $95 million in 2013, $362 million in 2014, and a whopping $866 million in 2015![1] Marc Andreesen, one of the world's most famous venture capitalists who has invested a lot of money into Bitcoin startup, wrote the following in 2014:

> Far from a mere libertarian fairy tale or a simple Silicon Valley exercise in hype, Bitcoin offers a sweeping vista of opportunity to reimagine how the financial system can and should work in the Internet era, and a catalyst to reshape that system in ways that are more powerful for individuals and businesses alike.[2]

While it is clear that cryptocurrencies are here to stay and have all kinds of disruptive potential, as I highlighted in Chapter 4, Bitcoin itself has lost many of its early supporters. Cass Sunstain, a legal theorist once coined the term polarization entrepreneurs which he described as being like terrorists in their dogmatic approach to a paradigm:

> They create enclaves of like-minded people. They stifle dissenting views and do not tolerate internal disagreement. They take steps to ensure a high degree of internal solidarity.[3]

According to many experts in the Bitcoin community,[4] one of the reasons Bitcoin has not reached mass market adoption is that some of the technologists in the Bitcoin community were exhibiting this type of polarization behavior and were inflexible with respect to adapting to the market in ways that would have allowed more mainstream citizens to embrace the currency. Yet, a powerful innovation that supported Bitcoin's introduction, the Blockchain, appears to be an enduring technology that will have transformative impacts on economies and society. Blockchain is a distributed ledger which permits anonymous users anywhere in the world to track asset ownership and exchange products and services, with cryptocurrency or alternative value transfer and exchange systems. As the Wall Street Journal reported:

> Today, more than 40 top financial institutions and a growing number of companies across industries are experimenting with distributed ledger technology as a trusted way to track the ownership of assets without the need for a central authority, which could speed up transactions and cut costs while lowering the chance of fraud.[5]

Blockchain is just one form of distributed ledger system to emerge. Ether is another cryptocurrency technology that uses a form of distributed ledger technology (DLT) usually referred to as Ethereum. Some technologists refer to blockchain as a generic term for all distributed ledger systems, whereas others specify which type of distributed ledger system is being employed and some group them all under the DLT tag.

Blockchain has significant potential to be the infrastructure layer, some refer to as web 3.0, to power all forms of distributed organizing including platform coops, the subject of Chapter 3, and of course DAOs which will be the focus of this chapter. Jamie Burke, a global expert on blockchain technology who leads an incubator and fund for blockchain startups in London, noted:

> Blockchains as decentralised systems; where networks of independent entities (be that people, machines or autonomous organisations) find

consensus by hard-coded rules (like proof-of-stake or proof-of-spend) or informal lobbying and democratic action (like hard forks) inherently operate by a process of collectivism whereby the underlying technology is effectively the commons.

It is no coincidence that all this happens at the same time as a revival in cooperativism be a new generation in places like Spain called "platform cooperativism." Where people are looking to new technologies to help better organise and extend the cooperative movement as an alternative model to capitalism. The challenge is coops have suffered from a tech deficit to VC backed capitalistic models but now with innovations such as the ICO communities can self-finance and maybe even out innovate corporations through open sourcing.

Given that blockhains/DLT will become the defacto standard for Web 3.0 across almost every industry it promises to represent a cultural shift away from monopolistic rent seeking models inherent to Web 2.0. Most VCs have stood on the sidelines watching how this plays out whilst the more brave are just making sure they have a seat at the table in the hope an opportunity arises. No one really knows how it will play out however my humble opinion is AIs hovering up all this lovely standardised data up will once again create monopolistic advantages in the long run. In many cases DLT is just the trojan horse.[6]

Distributed ledgers have the potential to transform or even disrupt most every industry, and even improve how democracies function. A recent working paper from the University of California Berkeley, identified at least eight areas of our economies and lives that could be improved through the application of blockchain technology: financial instruments and asset registries, nanopayments, identity management and online reputation, supply chain records and product-centric data, smart contracts, Internet of Things (IoT), voting systems, and DAOs.[7]

While all of these areas could be relevant to a discussion of PCE, I will focus briefly on smart contracts before focusing on DAOs. Smart contracts underlie much of the thinking of how blockchain could facilitate DAOs. As Vitalik Buterin, a cocreator of Etherum, noted, smart contracts could be transformative in enabling the elimination of traditional intermediaries, allowing DAOs to embed rules and trust into the code itself:

> what if, with the power of modern information technology, we can encode the mission statement into code; that is, create an inviolable contract that generates revenue, pays people to perform some function, and finds hardware for itself to run on, all without any need for top-down human direction?[8]

As Bettina Warburg, a global expert on blockchain stated in a recent Ted talk:

> Blockchains give us the technological capability of creating a record of human exchange, exchange of currency, of all kinds of physical and digital assets, even of our own personal attributes in a totally new way....We need to start preparing ourselves. Because we are about to face a world where distributed autonomous institutions have quite a significant role.[9]

My purpose here is not to go into more depth about how blockchain technology works or the range of applications for blockchain. There are entire books being written on this topic,* and I do not claim to be an expert on blockhain technology. Yet, what I am convinced of is that one powerful use case for blockchain technology is that it can support more PCE, in particular, serving as the foundational technology to permit the creation of DAOs.

SOME EARLY EXAMPLES OF DAOs

As I mentioned in the introduction, there are currently very few examples of DAOs in operation around the world. Here, I will draw on a few, even if their longevity is in doubt as they can help shed light on what might be possible, and also what challenges lie ahead for aspiring DAO models.

The D.A.O.

Without a doubt, the distributed autonomous organization that generated the most attention to date is actually called "The D.A.O." On April 30, 2016, The D.A.O. was launched with a goal of becoming a distributed investment vehicle for startups that embrace platform cooperative and alternative currency models. Amazingly, within a month, The D.A.O. had raised $150 million worth of cash and Ether commitments from 11,000 individual investors.[10] These early investors were taking a huge risk because there was so much unknown at the time of their investment, including if The D.A.O. was

---

* Some of the recent blockchain books include: *Blockchain: Blueprint for a New Economy* by Melanie Swan; *Blockchain Revolution* by Don Tapscott and his son, Alex Tapscott; and *The Science of the Blockchain*, by Roger Wattenhoffer.

even legal. The vision for The D.A.O. was to be a "sort of technology-enabled leaderless collective."[11] Even in the early days, many alternative currency and blockchain/ether experts offered doomsday predictions for the future of The D.A.O. Concerns raised early on were related to the vulnerability of the code itself, the legality of The D.A.O., and the difficulty in balancing the goals of a DAO seeking to become an alternative model for investing in PCEs where governance models were so democratic, given the amount of investment people were putting in to the project.

In fact, as The D.A.O. was wrapping up the largest crowdfunding round in history, three experts, including Emin Gun Sirer, a professor from Cornell University, issued a dire warning about the security vulnerabilities in the software driving The D.A.O. and made a call for a temporary moratorium while the vulnerabilities could be addressed.[12]

The D.A.O. had very lofty ideals such as being one of the first DAOs and by leveraging the idea of DAOs as an alternative type of democratized venture capital entity, whereby there would be no partners, no traditional corporate or heavyweight financial backers, not even a physical address. Instead, it would be run by a volunteer group of curators and the individual investors, primarily those who allocated ether to The D.A.O. would get voting rights regarding which projects to invest in.

Unfortunately, after such a massive success in their funding round, the experts who had identified numerous vulnerabilities in the code and the project proved to be right. In June of 2016, hackers recognized and exploited the vulnerabilities in the source code, and were able to siphon off about 1/3 or 50 million (USD equivalent) in Ether. This led to the demise of The D.A.O. project. However, interestingly, members from the Ether community:

> decided to…restore virtually all funds to the original contract. This was controversial, and led to a fork in Ethereum, where the original unforked blockchain was maintained as Ethereum Classic, thus breaking Ethereum into two separate active cryptocurrencies.[13]

In reflecting on the surprising rise, and expected fall of The D.A.O., Jamie Burke commented:

> The D.A.O in reality failed as a DAO not getting much further than a glorified escrow and a poor one at that but succeeded as an ICO (initial coin offerings). Actually it is the combination of both of these significant innovations of Web 3.0 that offers the holy-grail for blockheads and its really

just a matter of time before people correctly leverage them fully in concert. To be able to fund and then operate a commons without the need for middlemen is hugely powerful.

But in my opinion it's safe to say we should expect a lot of failed experimentation along the way largely because those driving the innovation are often idealists who still subscribe to libertarian cyberpunk principles and believe in total decentralisation and tenets such as "code is law." They only have an agenda of disruption which inhibits the kind of pragmatism that will bring about a more transformative wave of innovation to industry.[6]

The D.A.O. project was obviously very ambitious and certainly raised awareness for the potential and some of the pitfalls that must be mitigated when trying to develop a DAO. Let's look at another emerging DAO model with perhaps more potential to last.

Open Bazaar

eBay may be one of the first early successes in the peer-to-peer economy. Founded in 1995 in Silicon Valley by Pierre Omidyar, eBay is a classical Silicon Valley success story. As most readers will know, eBay got its start by facilitating peer-to-peer transactions for new and used goods regardless of geographic location. eBay was one of the first digital companies to demonstrate it was possible to build trust via a digital, virtual platform to enable transactions among geographically dispersed strangers. While eBay is rarely discussed in terms of being part of the sharing economy, perhaps because eBay's founding and growth preceded our modern definition of the space, eBay really was a pioneer in the creation of an intermediated P2P platform. Yet, like other later players such as Airbnb, eBay profits significantly from these transactions. In 2016, eBay generated $9 billion in revenue and more than 7.2 billion in net income.[14]

Open Bazaar was formed to compete with the eBay model by facilitating similar transactions among peers, but with no intermediary monetizing the transactions. So, what is Open Bazaar and how does it challenge the status quo created by eBay? In their own words:

> OpenBazaar is an open source project to create a decentralized network for peer to peer commerce online—using Bitcoin—that has no fees and no restrictions...
>
> OpenBazaar is a different approach to online commerce. It puts the power back in the users' hands. Instead of buyers and sellers going through

a centralized service, OpenBazaar connects them directly. Because there is no one in the middle of your transactions there are no fees, no restrictions, no accounts to create, and you only reveal the personal information that you choose.[15]

The OpenBazaar model is unique in that it operates as a DAO, leveraging open-source software and the open, distributed currency of Bitcoin. Yet, OpenBazaar obtained its first financing round of US$1 million in June 2015 from Silicon Valley stalwarts, Andressen Horowitz and Union Square. When I first learned of this, I was personally thrown off. How could a venture capitalist invest in a DAO directly when the nature of a DAO is that it is not an organization or company and is not an intermediary? I explored more inquiring with some of my colleagues in the DAO movement and through further research I realized they have a unique model.

Originally, the primary developers of the open-source software for OpenBazaar were not even seeking investment. Yet, when some of Silicon Valley's heavy hitters showed interest, Brian Hoffman, the lead developer of OpenBazaar couldn't resist. He formed a private company, OB1, to receive the investment which will be focused on trying to monetize optional-value-added services such as escrow accounts or shopfronts. This is in line with Hoffman's view that platforms should not try to take part in every transaction from small businesses and peers in P2P transactions, and instead seek other ways to generate revenue through optional-value-added services:

> I think the decentralised model where "take rates" (the percentage cut the marketplace takes) are eliminated will force the incumbents to have to rethink their strategy for capturing profit from consumers. It will force them to have to think about new ways to provide value-added services rather than just raising fees on customers to make more money.[16]

This may remind some readers of the Aquapioneers discussion from Chapter 1 about commons-based peer production where the founders are committed to the commons for their digital aquaponics product, but are exploring other revenue models for additional value-added services they can provide to interested makers, users, small businesses, and even school districts. Yet, the difference here is that OpenBazaar is essentially a DAO and OB1 is a firm that will own no rights over the software whatsoever since it is an open-source project. Instead, OB1 aims to be a first mover in the development and delivery for optional-value-added services that can be added to the platform.

Interestingly, just 6 months after closing its first funding round, OB1 was able to receive another US$3 million in investment. But this time, from a different investment source. BlueYard Capital, a Berlin-based VC firm, only invests in projects aimed to disrupt centralized intermediated platform models with more open, distributed approaches. BlueYard's founders believe that the Amazon's, eBay's, and Airbnb's of the world:

> have terms, algorithms and pricing structures (that) can put merchants and buyers at a significant disadvantage. They (the likes of Amazon and eBay) can also lock out merchants and buyers that happen to be outside of their scope of operations.
>
> There is no gatekeeper that can influence who can participate in the marketplace, what goods are sold and at what price. There is no central entity that can dictate search/ranking algorithms, control data of merchants and buyers, or charge any fees.[17]

A DAO for Uber or Airbnb?

Uber and Airbnb are the platform deathstars that draw the most attention and ire from certain stakeholders around the world. And believe me, there are many PCEs and technologists aiming to disrupt their monopolistic and often predatory business models. Recently, I had a chance to speak with Sito Veracruz, cofounder of the Amsterdam-based urban consultancy, Citymakers. Veracruz told me that Citymakers has a proposal with a nonprofit, Faircity Amsterdam, and The Waag Society to create a DAO to offer a competitive vacation-rental platform as part of the broader Fairbnb movement. Their goal is to create:

> a local short-stay platform. We aim to elaborate a responsible vacational platform in line with the needs and regulations of the city and self-managed by citizens. The idea behind this project is to foster the decentralization of tourism management and leave part of the responsibility to the neighbors, who are able to take profits from it.

Citymakers is preparing a pitch to a Netherlands program called SINDS Blockchain for Good which would help finance the early beta version of the platform. When I pressed him for more details about their plans for making this a DAO, he confessed they are still in the early stages of revising their plans:

> We are sure that we will use blockchain for identity verification purposes, but we still need to figure out what to do about the blockchain-supported payments. We don't know whether we will try to introduce smart contracts in this first phase (I doubt it because it is really expensive) or if we will use cryptocurrencies for p2p payments and eventually for supporting social projects.[18]

His cost concerns are primarily related to programming costs for smart contracts because of the limited number of programmers with smart contracts expertise at this juncture. Of course, we discussed ensuring this to be a full open-source project, whereby global programming experts could collaborate in the development of this DAO as an alternative to Airbnb. Perhaps, there are possibilities to combine DAOs with ICOs (from Chapter 4) as a way to fund the development and maintenance of the DAO. Or like we saw with the case of OpenBazaar, and we have witnessed over time with Linux, there are ample opportunities to develop revenue-generating businesses that support open-source projects.

PLATFORMS FOR DAOs

Just as Mondragon has become a network to support multiple traditional cooperatives around the globe, new initiatives are emerging to support the development of DAOs. Of course, most of them fully embrace DAO principles of openness, smart contracts, and alternative currencies in their own development as well. Here, I will highlight a few of these DAO platforms.*

Slock.it

Simon and Christoph Jentzsch and Stephan Tual founded Slock.it in Mittweida, Germany, with the goal of supporting the growth of DAOs around the world through the creation of an open-source platform. Christoph Jentzsch, by the way, is credited with creating the original code

---

* Note if you want to stay up to date on the latest news and developments in the DAO space, the DAOhub is like an open wiki fórum for such discussions https://forum.daohub.org.

for The D.A.O. discussed earlier in this chapter. Slock.it envisions a new type of sharing economy where peers can "rent, sell, or share anything without middlemen." This of course is the promise of DAOs, backed by distributed ledgers and smart contracts. Slock.it has embraced open-source code, making their DAO code free for use and improvement by anyone.

While it does not appear that Slock.it has a direct revenue strategy associated with their open-source DAO platform, their founders are leveraging their expertise in blockchain and DAO to advise and work with a range of corporate clients. For example, they are working with energy producers exploring distributed energy models and automotive manufacturers developing autonomous fleet technology for self-driving taxis.

> Our technology connects the blockchain to the physical world, effectively giving connected objects an identity, the ability to receive payments and the capability to enter complex agreements.

Divvy DAO

The Slock.it team is not alone in recognizing the value of creating an open-source platform that could be optimized and used by a range of different DAOs. The Divvy platform being developed:

> will provide the tools that decentralized autonomous organizations (DAOs) require to be efficient, effective, and resilient, setting goals and establishing tasks in any enterprise while rewarding those putting forth the effort in completing those tasks.[19]

At the time of writing, Divvy DAO was quite nascent but had big ambitions to develop several open tools for the DAO community, including a VOIP chat server, supporting the Etherium Cooperative in developing a host of ethereum applications, a community token exchange, and even virtual reality tools, among others.[20]

FROM DISTRIBUTED ORGANIZATIONS TO DISTRIBUTED NATIONS?

Much of the criticism about the flaws of capitalism has been directed toward the private sector with respect to exploitation of labor and the planet for financial gain. Yet, many advocates of a post-capitalist society suggest that multilateral, national, and even local governments are also to blame for the current inequalities and ecological challenges. Much of the critique of government comes from those concerned about the ubiquitous and prevalent corruptibility of governments. The World Economic Forum reports that the cost of corruption is equivalent to approximately 5% of global GDP, that is, US$2.6 trillion.[21] Lobbyists, kickbacks, and other mechanisms have been used by the private sector to influence laws and regulations for the benefit of private corporations instead of citizens' well-being. Even when corruption is not directly involved, there is still the reality that the privatization of the commons (see Chapter 1) leads to enclosures of land and resources supposedly for use by all citizens.

Many PCEs are not just directing their angst toward the private sector but are also trying to build models that change the dynamics of the private–public sector by giving more power to the people. In fact, the rise of cryptocurrencies such as Bitcoin largely coincided with the Occupy Movement and the perception that the "system is rigged" with banks "too big to fail." Recently, some have suggested that DAOs could even be used to disintermediate and disrupt not only private banks but even federal and regional banks like the European Central Bank.[22] Furthermore, technology-enabled global citizens have been collaborating to build DAOs that could challenge the role and power of nation states. *Bitnation*, for example, is a "Decentralized Borderless Voluntary Nation powered by Ethereum blockchain." Founded by Susanne Tarkowski Tempelhof, Bitnation to

> foster a peer-to-peer voluntary governance system, rather than the current "top-down," "one-size-fits-all" model, restrained by the current nation-state engineered geographical apartheid, where your quality of life is defined by where you were arbitrarily born.[23]

Bitnation aims to create a borderless global nation to counteract the inequalities around the globe by allowing people to choose their own social, economic, and governance system within the blockchain-enabled, borderless Bitnation.

> Bitnation has organized the world's first blockchain marriage, the world's first blockchain land-titles, the world's first blockchain birth certificate, the world's first official partnership between a virtual nation and a traditional nation, and deployed the world's first virtual nation constitution. We're a holacratic organization and we strive to become a fully functional

Decentralized Autonomous Organization (DAO). In non-geek terms, this means that there are no formal management structures, there are no barriers to entry, and everyone can join and create their own operational centers ("holons") whether for-profit or nonprofit, or join an existing one, all while benefiting from the greater support and technology from the BITNATION community.

At the moment, Bitnation has a platform whereby citizens around the globe can make proposals for new projects ranging from alternative forms of blockchain-enabled local governance (e.g., crypto-powered energy grid, DAO governed vertical farming), global governance (e.g., third-party insurance, peer-to-peer security system), and infrastructure (i.e., enhancing the Bitnation infrastructure). While Bitnation may seem a bit utopian and far-fetched, aside from attracting civil society, it has also begun to make traction with actual nation states.

At the Brainbar futures conference in Budapest I had the pleasure to speak with Estonia's former President Ilves about his government's pioneering approaches to digital democracy. Estonia is one of the most advanced countries in facilitating online transactions for almost any government service through their e-residency program. Even non-citizens or residents of Estonia can actually obtain an e-residency status with Estonia, allowing them, for example, to create an Estonian-based startup in just 24 hours and manage it from anywhere in the world using Estonian banks via online access. In 2015, the Government of Estonia announced a partnership with Bitnation to offer notarization services for marriages, birth certificates, and business contracts to e-residents.

> In Estonia we believe that people should be able to freely choose their digital/public services best fit to them, regardless of the geographical area where they were arbitrarily born. We're truly living in exciting times when nation states and virtual nations compete and collaborate with each other on an international market, to provide better governance services.[24] (Kaspar Korjus, Estonia e-Residency Program Director)

THE FUTURE FOR DAOs

It is hard not to be skeptical about DAOs because there is so little traction about them to date, because their underlying model assumes participants in the creation of DAOs are committed to the commons and not their own self-interest, and of course because the largest experiment in DAOs to date, The D.A.O., crashed hard and fast after its meteoric rise and after raising $150 million worth of alternative currency. Yet, at the same time, DAOs represent a promise of an economic model with no monetizing, monopolistic intermediary usurping the value of assets and time shared between peers on platforms. DAOs, in my opinion, suggest a powerful alternative to venture-capital-backed platform capitalists (or deathstars if you will) and could really democratize economic activity, enabling those who create real value to obtain fair compensation in return.

Recently, I had a conversation with a taxi driver on my way to the Barcelona airport. In Barcelona, Uber is outlawed, so many use alternative taxi-haling services such as Hailo and My Taxi. Both of these services rely on the existing regulated fleet of taxi drivers but add Uber-style location-based services to locate a nearby taxi and to execute payments via the application. I discovered on this particular ride that Hailo, my preferred app in Barcelona, charges 10% of the fare. Perhaps, at first this may not sound like a lot, given the investment in technology and marketing that firms like Hailo have made to scale their service. But to this taxi driver, whose margins are extremely thin, Hailo's share of my trip wipes out much of his net income. He told me he and some of his taxi-driving friends were exploring developing their own app to eliminate Hailo as a middle man. This caused me to reflect on the dozens of taxi drivers I have met in my life who have Ph.Ds or master's in computer science and engineering and I thought, wow, this group could organize on a global level, create either a platform coop, or even better, a DAO, eliminating any intermediaries, allowing the taxi drivers to make a better living similar to what Denver's Green Taxi drivers did.

> Perversely DLT offers a challenge to the state such as Bitcoin but at the same time the best tool Governments have ever had to have total audibility of a cashless society. If offers both the ability for top down innovation, such as cities providing compliant DLT for a true sharing economy to counter disruptive elements, or bottom up such as ex-Uber drivers forming decentralised driver coops. It provides a real counter to stateless ultra-capitalistic tech companies but arguably provides a parallel state devoid of citizenship and effective tax systems.[6]

I do believe somehow, some form of DAOs or something similar will emerge in the next 5–10 years, empowering value creators to optimize their efforts without the coercive or monopolistic behavior of platform capitalists and possibly challenging the power of nation states as well. DAOs may have a global developer base and global reach while also embedding smart contracts and hyperlocal features and services. Time will tell, but if they do take off, DAOs would radically transform our economies to allow value creators to obtain all of the value for their services without deathstars intermediating their transactions. In Chapter 6, I will challenge the prevailing wisdom that venture capital is a necessary condition for supporting a vibrant entrepreneurial community, especially in the world of post-capitalist entrepreneurship.

REFERENCES

1. Blockchain Venture Capital, Coindesk, http://www.coindesk.com/bitcoin-venture-capital/#. Accessed February 2017.
2. Marc Andressen, Why Bitcoin Matters, *The New York Times*, January 2014, https://dealbook.nytimes.com/2014/01/21/why-bitcoin-matters/. Accessed February 2017.
3. Cass Sunstein, 2002. Why they hate us: The role of social dyanmics, *Harvard Journal of Law & Public Policy* 429.
4. Timothy Lee, Bitcoin was Supposed to Change the World. What happened? Vox. com, November 2016, http://www.vox.com/new-money/2016/11/21/13669662/bitcoin-ethereum-future-explained. Accessed February 2017.
5. Steve Norton, CIO Explainer: What is Blockchain? *The Wall Street Journal*, February 2016, http://blogs.wsj.com/cio/2016/02/02/cio-explainer-what-is-blockchain/. Accessed February 2017.
6. Private conversations with Jamie Burke in February/March 2017.
7. Juri Mattila, The Blockchain Phenomenon, Berkeley Roundtable on the International Economy, Working Paper, 2016, http://www.brie.berkeley.edu/wp-content/uploads/2015/02/Juri-Mattila-.pdf. Accessed January 2017.
8. Ellie Rennie and Jason Potts, The DAO: a radical experiment that could be the future of decentralized governance. The Conversation, May 2016, http://theconversation.com/the-dao-a-radical-experiment-that-could-be-the-future-of-decentralised-governance-59082. Accessed January 2017.
9. Bettina Warburg, How the Blockchain will Radically Transform the Economy, *TED Talk*, June 2016, https://www.ted.com/talks/bettina_warburg_how_the_blockchain_will_radically_transform_the_economy#t-817417. Accessed February 2017.
10. Nathaniel Porter, A Venture Fund with Plenty of Virtual Capital but No Capitalist, *The New York Times*, May 2016, https://www.nytimes.com/2016/05/22/business/dealbook/crypto-ether-bitcoin-currency.html?_r=1. Accessed February 2017.
11. Nathaniel Porter, A Venture Fund with Plenty of Virtual Capital but No Capitalist, *The New York Times*, May 2016, https://www.nytimes.com/2016/05/22/business/dealbook/crypto-ether-bitcoin-currency.html?_r=1. Accessed February 2017.
12. Dino Mark, Vlad Zamfir and Emin Gun Sirer, A Call for a Temporary Moratorium on The DAO. Hacking Distributed, May 2016, http://hackingdistributed.com/2016/05/27/dao-call-for-moratorium/. Accessed February 2017.

13. The DAO, Wikipedia, https://en.wikipedia.org/wiki/The_DAO_(organization)# Operation. Accessed February 2017.
14. NASDAQ: eBay, Google Finance, https://www.google.com/finance?q=NASDAQ%3 AEBAY&fstype=ii&ei=H9T4UPi ZFMrqkAWb5QE. Accessed April 2017.
15. Open Bazaar Homepage https://blog.openbazaar.org/what-is-openbazaar/#.WKr-MXeZOqA. Accessed February 2017.
16. Rob Price, Some of Tech's Biggest Investors are Funding a Police-Proof Marketplace that lets you Sell Literally Anything, Business Insider, June 2015, http://uk.businessinsider.com/openbazaar-gets-1-million-seed-round-from-andreessen-horowitz-union-square-ventures-2015-6. Accessed November 2016.
17. Philipp Banhardt and Chad Fowler, OB1 & OpenBazaar, Medium, December 2016, https://medium.com/@BlueYard/ob1-openbazaar-2be35862e0bf#.mqmgwnpn5. Accessed January 2017.
18. Private conversations with Sito Veracruz in February 2017.
19. DivvyDAO Homepage, http://divvydao.org, Accessed February 2017.
20. Brent, DivvyDAO-Collaborative DAO Project Building the Stepping Stones to Social Adaption in the Cryptoeconomy, DivvyDAO.org, July 2016, http://divvydao.org/index.php/2016/07/08/divvydao-collaborative-dao-project-building-the-stepping-stones-to-social-adaption-in-the-cryptoeconomy/, Accessed February 2017.
21. The Rationale for Fighting Corruption, OECD 2014, https://www.oecd.org/cleangovbiz/49693613.pdf. Accessed November 2016.
22. Benedikt Herudek, Can the European Central Bank go DAO? How Blockchain will Help Europe, Coin Telegraph, May 2016, https://cointelegraph.com/news/can-the-european-central-bank-go-dao-how-blockchain-will-help-europe. Accessed December 2016.
23. Bitnation: Geographical Apartheid, Youtube, October 2016, https://www.youtube.com/watch?v=j3Nkol6MGVo. Accessed January 2017.
24. Giulio Prisco, Estonian Government Partners with Bitnation to Offer Blockchain Notarization Services to e-Residents, Bitcoin Magazine, November 2015, https://bitcoinmagazine.com/articles/estonian-government-partners-with-bitnation-to-offer-blockchain-notarization-services-to-e-residents -1448915243/. Accessed January 2017.

6

Venture Capital is Dead in a PCE World

Winner-take-all capitalism will remain a driver, especially in the United States but is increasingly at odds with the 99% movement. When entrepreneurs are no longer driven to own the world, the venture capital model no longer applies. How will startups be financed in a post-capitalist entrepreneurship (PCE) world? In this chapter, I will explore a range of emerging alternatives to venture capital for financing startups with a strong focus on a range of crowdfunding platforms. I will also discuss the growing slow money movement and impact investors who seek to invest in enterprises with a strong social and environmental mandate. Also, I will discuss ways in which civic entrepreneurs are funding their projects through procurement for innovation programs from local and regional governments as well as explore how the alternative currency movement can connect to startup finance more directly.

BACKGROUND ON THE VENTURE CAPITAL INDUSTRY

I must confess, for many years, like many in the entrepreneurship community, I was enthralled by the venture capital world and Silicon Valley. I obtained my PhD in entrepreneurship at the University of Colorado in Boulder which to some extent aspired to be like Silicon Valley. In fact, my first ever research project during my doctoral program was exploring what factors drove the success of Boulder's technology ecosystem and what role the venture capital community played.[1] Furthermore, the focus of my doctoral dissertation was on exploring the explosion of dot.com startups in the late 1990s and what factors influenced their venture capital funding and eventual valuations when they issued their initial public offerings (IPOs).

Years later, in 2008, I had my first chance to visit Silicon Valley. Not as a researcher, but as a startup founder. I had a startup called 3rdWhale which was developing mobile applications for the green consumer, with our primary service focusing on a location-based application to facilitate connections between green consumers and local green/ethical retailers and service providers. I was selected through a Canadian government program (I was living in Vancouver at the time) to pitch my startup at an event with major venture capitalists being hosted at a well-known incubator/accelerator space in the Valley, Plug and Play. Along with 45 other aspiring entrepreneurs from around the world, we first did a lightning round of 2-minute pitches with the top five being selected for a larger pitch, in front of the likes of Tim Draper, a partner in the acclaimed venture capital firm, Draper Fisher Jurvetson. After being selected in the top five, I was so enthusiastic about 3rdWhale's chances to raise money in the Valley that the same day I signed up to have shared office space in Plug and Play.

Over the next year, I travelled once a month to meet with venture capitalists to explore potential investment. One of my meetings with a venture capital firm during this period opened my eyes to the realization that traditional venture capital would not work for 3rdWhale. In this meeting, the investors said they liked our original location-based application but in order to consider investing we would have to reframe our company not as a green app company but a location-based app developer with our first app being focused on green consumers. The investor may have been right that our approach was not scalable enough for venture capitalists, but our core values of the founding team (as I was pitching the company to investors, I was able to bring on a cofounder who had sold his prior company for 17 million (USD) and was as committed to sustainability as I was) were not malleable just because it might be better for scalability.

It was because of this experience that I began to question the venture capital model. From my own experiences as an entrepreneur, it seemed that in general, venture capitalists were more focused on profit maximization at all costs instead of real value creation or social impact. Since then, my critique of the venture capital industry has only grown. As I wrote in my 2016 book[2]:

> The tech boom of the latter twentieth century was largely financed by venture capitalists who take big risks in the hopes of big returns. In fact, the

venture capital model generally assumes that only one of every 10 investments generates returns. But for the model to work, that one successful investment needs to return at least a 10× return on initial investment. A $10 million venture capital investment in a start-up, say in 1995, was hoped to generate a return of $100 million by 2000. This of course puts significant pressure on venture-backed start-up CEOs to scale their company fast and ideally find an exit within 5 years of venture financing.

David Heinemeier Hansson, cofounder of Basecamp, an online project management tool, railed against the venture capital model in a 2015 blog post stating: "I wanted to put down roots. Long term bonds with coworkers and customers and the product. Impossible to steer and guide with a VC timebomb ticking that can only be defused by a 10–100× return."

As my colleague, Pablo Muñoz and I recently concluded, venture capital often takes entrepreneurs out of synch with their communities and the natural environment.[3] Even if we consider, for example, B Corps, the subject of Chapter 2, which still operate within our market system, one could envision significant challenges for such purpose-driven entrepreneurs to obtain, and be in synch with, venture capitalist expectation of growth and firm exit. In fact, from the dozens, if not hundreds, of purpose-driven entrepreneurs I have interviewed and met with over the past several years, the idea of an exit (selling the venture to a larger firm or going public) seems to be very low on the priority list. I do not have the data to confirm this, but I suspect venture capital has played a disproportionately smaller role in financing B Corps than other firms of similar size operating in the same industries. The conflicts of the two paradigms: maximizing profit in the short term from investing in highly scalable businesses with a good chance of exit, with the values of purpose-driven entrepreneurs to have lasting impact on communities and the environment are obviously not well aligned.

Dan Lyons, a writer and also former employee of HubSpot, had some harsh words about venture capital at the 2017 South by Southwest technology conference in Austin, Texas:

The VC-backed business model tech companies follow now is "grow fast, lose money, go public, cash out...The VC industry has become less diverse and more influential," Lyons said. "The VC industry is bunch of bros and they invest in brothers (i.e. white males)."[4]

So if purpose-driven, but market entrepreneurs such as those with B Corp certification are out of synch with venture capitalist expectations, imagine the disconnect with other PCEs I have discussed throughout this book like commons-based peer production, platform cooperatives, alternative currencies, and DAOs.

IS VENTURE CAPITAL REALLY DEAD IN A PCE WORLD?

I am not so naïve to suggest that there will be no room for venture capitalists in the future. In 2015, more than US$77 billion was allocated by venture capitalists in the US alone,[5] with estimates that global venture capital investing will grow 35% a year through 2020.[6] Some evidence suggests that early-stage startup funding may dry up faster than follow-on investing for firms on the path to becoming, or already are, unicorns, valued at $1 billion or more. But as the famous entrepreneur, Steve Case, founder of America Online (AOL) and investor, recently documented, we may be heading for a time with fewer such rocket startups and more smaller startups that never reach such scale.[7] So there may always be a role for venture capital, especially in market economy startups. Even in a PCE world, there appears to be opportunities for venture capital at times.

As I have already documented in this book, some PCE-type projects have received venture capital financing. Certainly, the cryptocurrency space has received several billion in venture capital funding although not all cryptocurrency projects are squarely in the PCE world, for example, those that seek to support the traditional banking industry. Meanwhile, others such as Colu, the local cryptocurrency startup in Israel, have had success raising venture capital, in part because they are also working with governments in the developing world to modernize their central banking system with cryptocurrency. Similarly, the lead developers behind OpenBazaar were also able to raise a few rounds of venture capital investment, albeit the latter round being led by an alternative venture capital firm in Germany seeking to invest in distributed models. So, the short answer to my question is "no, not really." Venture capital will continue to have a role to play in the traditional market economy for a long time to come, and in some instances, will even help fund a few scalable enterprises focused more in the PCE world. But these examples may be few and far between.

The overwhelming majority of PCEs will either not be funded at all, or will be funded via alternative approaches to what the venture capital industry offers. The rest of this chapter is focused on such alternatives emerging for developing and funding PCEs without venture capital.

FINANCING ALTERNATIVES FOR PCEs

Before discussing alternative financing solutions, it is important to recognize that the world of innovation and entrepreneurship is already changing significantly. As I documented in great detail in my 2016 book, we have been experiencing a transformation in the cost and accessibility of tools for innovators. The democratization of tools for innovating, everything from the explosion of coworking spaces reducing the need for paying for office space, to software as a service (SaaS) permitting inexpensive access to software tools, Fab Labs and 3D printing offering the possibility for makers to tinker, experiment, and test new products without having to build or rent manufacturing facilities, and cloud computing putting servers in the cloud for use on demand instead of having to purchase and maintain in-house servers. This has led experts to conclude that many startups will no longer need access to venture capital to grow their ventures. Combining low-cost access to the tools of innovation with the rapid growth of design thinking and lean startup methodologies, which encourage rapid prototyping with real users and validating demand before spending much money, means that many small- and medium-sized startups may be able to self-finance or generate enough early revenue to survive without seeking venture capital.

Of course, that all applies to startups operating in the traditional market economy but is just as relevant, if not, more so for PCEs. First of all, reflecting back on the discussions regarding commons-based peer production, PCEs may rely on the goodwill of the community through a commitment to open-source models, whereby everyone can contribute to the development and improvement of a product, software, or service, while also benefitting from that development without money having to change hands at all. Yet, there will continue to be PCEs seeking some form of financing to make their dreams come true. Since venture capital is not likely the best option, or even viable at all, how will PCEs obtain the financing they need? Here are some emerging options worth exploring in more depth.

Crowdfunding

Crowdfunding has emerged in recent years as a powerful force that has demonstrated the power of more distributed models for our economy.

Even in the market economy, where most crowdfunding platforms operate, the crowdfunding model by nature is distributed and generally peer to peer. Instead of relying on a single, or a few, angel investors or venture capital firms to invest in an enterprise, crowdfunding allows aspiring entrepreneurs the opportunity to gain access to needed financial resources from the crowd. There are numerous types of crowdfunding models, such as peer-to-peer lending, equity-based crowdfunding, and what is commonly referred to as rewards-based crowdfunding.* Across all these types, in 2015, 34 billion (USD) was raised globally via crowdfunding platforms with $25 billion going for P2P lending, $5.5 billion in reward-based crowdfunding, and $2.5 billion in equity-based crowdfunding.[8] Crowdfunding is likely to not just have a continuing impact in the developed world but also could reach nearly 100 billion (USD) annually by 2038.[9]

In the world of PCEs, I believe crowdfunding is going to be the primary financing model going forward. The distributed nature of crowdfunding is highly synergistic with the values shared by PCEs. Also, given that virtually all PCEs explored in this book rely on democratic models with peer contributions, the potential for the very same peers to also consider financing the project they support via crowdfunding is substantial. For example, Peerby, the Dutch sharing platform, leveraged the crowdfunding platform OnePlanetCrowd to raise more than 1.7 million (euros) in just one weekend in March 2016, from more than 1,000 investors, most of whom were Peerby users. One Peerby member, Jeroen Segers, who contributed to the crowdfunding campaign explained his rationale for the investment:

> I invested in Peerby because I believe in the dream and in the team. We need a smarter organisation of the way we use and own items and Peerby is well equipped in finding an answer. As an investor I also look carefully at the people behind the organisation. I know them for a while and I believe in this team, in the past they have shown that there approach is resourceful.[10]

---

* In recent years, several books have been published which detail these different types of crowdfunding as well as providing detailed suggestions for aspiring entrepreneurs on how to build a successful campaign. *Crowdfunding: The Next Big Thing* by Gary Spirer and *The Crowdfunding Revolution: How to Raise Venture Capital Using Social Media* by Kevin Lawton and Dan Marom are a couple of good examples. Also, in my entrepreneurship courses, I use a case about MilkMade Icecream out of New York City, which details the strategies employed by the founder and her colleague to strategically reach their crowdfunding campaign targets. This case is entitled: *Milkmade Ice Cream: Running a Successful Crowdfunding Campaign* (UV6995).

Also, it is important to note that the growth in cryptocurrency also facilitates distributed crowdfunding models by allowing the average citizen to invest in projects even easier than before, minimizing the need for aggregated funds managed by venture capital firms.

> We can invest in a decentralized platform as a seed investor when they first release their crypto-currency. It is pure crowdfunding. With as little as a few dollars, you can participate and be an investor in a disrupting technology.
> There is no minimal buy-in because transaction costs are almost none. The absence of Bank and institution regulating and processing the transaction make that possible.[11]

Of course, as we saw in the last chapter with the case of The D.A.O., there remain many risks to distributed, crypto-based crowdfunding platforms for investment. But, as is the case for virtually every disruptive innovation introduced in society, there is a learning curve that often involves some failures before the successes emerge.

Civic Crowdfunding

While PCEs could use potentially any crowdfunding platform for their projects, I would expect to see most PCEs seeking to work with platforms and funders that share their values. Civic crowdfunding platforms like Neighbor.ly (US), Voor je Buurt (The Netherlands), and Spacehive (UK) are a few of the growing number of crowdfunding platforms devoted to enabling local citizens and community groups to fund projects to improve their own neighborhoods, and are certainly of appeal to local PCEs.

Kickstarter

Even Kickstarter, the world's largest and most visible crowdfunding platform, has high values alignment with PCEs. In 2014, Kickstarter solidified its commitment by reincorporating as a benefit corporation and becoming a B corp. In their Benefit Corporation Charter, Kickstarter makes several tangible commitments to a beyond-profit model such as donating 5% of after-tax profits to a range of causes such as arts and music education and reducing systemic inequality, investing in green infrastructure, and to never sell user data to third parties.

Goteo

In Chapter 1, I introduced Goteo, a crowdfunding platform founded in Spain with a visionary commitment to the principles of open democratic governance and supporting projects that share their commitment to the commons. Goteo is committed to ensuring that all crowdfunding projects develop collective incentives which generate a social return for society.

On Goteo, at any given time, you can find technologists, environmentalists, artists, and makers seeking to fund projects that will give back to their communities and perhaps in their own way, also be generative. At the time of writing, for example, Ecotxe had raised more than 12,000 euros from 121 backers (with a 10,500 euro goal minimum for the campaign) to help form an electric car share cooperative in Mallorca, Spain.

Based in Sevilla, Spain, Sin Cadenas (without chains in English) has raised more than 6,500 euros for a program focused on bridging the bicycle divide associated with adult women in the city who have never learned to ride a bike. Founded by Isabel Porras, an urban mobility activist, Fernando Martinez and Gonzalo Bueno Gomez, professional bike mechanics; Manuel Calvo, an environmental consultant; Elena Huerta, an anthropologist; and Edro Benitez Arvez, a former Paraguayan national champion mountain biker, Sin Cadenas has trained 300 women so far and with the funding campaign aims to amplify their impact via a physical and digital express guide, adding new in-person classes and the acquisition of recycled and repaired bikes in order to gift them to lower income women seeking to get on a bike of their own in Sevilla.

I have had the pleasure of numerous interactions with two of the founders of Goteo, Enric Senabre and Olivier Schulbaum in recent years. In a recent dialogue with Enric, I asked him what they see on the horizon as transformational changes in the Goteo model. He quickly responded, their matching funding program. While I had heard of it, I admit I had not yet recognized the importance of the matching funding program. So I asked him to describe the program and explain why it could be revolutionary. The text below is excerpted and edited from my conversations with Enric.

Since 2013, Goteo has been a pioneer in recruiting public/private capital investors to help develop open and civic-oriented projects through a bottom-up process, beyond crowdfunding defaults, in a "match-funding" scheme, where each euro a project receives from an individual is matched by another euro from institutions within a social investment fund. Through specific calls (driven by themes of public interest like education, sustainability, culture, etc.), Goteo channels private and public organizations to invest in common-based initiatives by matching funds raised from the crowd. This way investing organizations (universities, local governments, local innovation agencies) can give wings to some of their areas of concern and their programs in an innovative way, as well as to their political obligations and social responsibilities.

Leveraging the matchfunding program, Goteo Foundation seeks to set the standard of a matchfunding system where public money and resources progressively multiply donations from civil society. By bringing in nontraditional players like public administration to the social economy and the commons field, one of the main objectives of this type of matchfunding is to improve efficiency and fairness in public funding and resources, while creating policy standards to promote hybrid formulas of collaboration and support between public and private agents.

Goteo's matchfunding programs have a clear "multiplier" effect. To start with, the credibility of the crowdfunded project increases when it has the institution's hallmark, receiving the trust of the community and thus has a better chance of attracting crowd donations. The more crowdfunds received, the higher the matching contribution by the institution, the bigger the total project budget becomes. Goteo's data show that a crowdfunding campaign with institutional support receives on average 180% more from crowd donations than a campaign without institutional support. Also, its success probability (reaching the minimum set campaign budget) is increased up to 90% (in comparison with Goteo's 71% success rate for campaigns without match funding).

Goteo Foundation has conducted 12 match funding calls with different institutions, gathering more than 200,000 euros and valuable open data, which enable knowledge about matchfunding for projects to build broader communities, and for match funder organizations to communicate the benefits and impact of this hybrid funding model.

LOCAL INVESTMENT CLUBS

The Cooperative Principal is a different type of investment club. It was started in Minneapolis with 17 members who all contributed a $99 (USD) one-time membership fee, and another $50 per month to advise and invest in local cooperatives. To date, the first club has invested over 10,000 (USD) in a handful of cooperatives in food and finance. Like most PCEs discussed throughout this book, the Cooperative Principal is committed to contributing their expertise and resources to a global commons. The Cooperative Principal is keen to spread their model "investment clubs for the 99%. 100% dedicated to co-ops" to supporting communities around the globe in adopting this model. Cooperative Principal has posted a PDF on their website which offers 13 tips for starting a local investment club.[12] In their own words, the beauty of the Cooperative Principal model is that:

> people who on their own can't afford to invest in their values now have a vehicle to do so and co-ops have access to a new source of capital. Beyond the dollars and cents, there is a social and educational component to The Cooperative Principal. Members meet in person a minimum of 4 times per year, ideally in a social setting (think microbrewery!) and the clubs operate in a cooperative, democratic manner. Based on investment analysis from the central non-profit, or their own research, members discuss and vote on where to put their pooled funds. Club members are both participating in their own democratic organizations and supporting the co-op economy in a way that is only possible by working together.

Since launching the first club, Cooperative Principal has assisted the launch of new clubs in Vermont, Massachusetts, and Michigan, with new clubs to come in Wisconsin and North Carolina with US$60,000 in assets; 60 total members and 17 cooperatives have received funding from the clubs.[13]

ICOs AS DISRUPTIVE FORCE FOR FINANCING STARTUPS

In Chapter 4, I introduced initial coin offerings (ICOs). There is growing interest in ICOs not just to support the creation of new alternative currencies but potentially as an alternative to raising capital for technology startups as well. In fact, coindesk.com went so far as to state that 2016 was "the year blockchain ICOs disrupted venture capital".[14] Justification was based on the rapid growth of ICOs as a tool for startup fundraising in 2016. According to their research, not including the spectacular rise and fall of The DAO (Chapter 5), 2016 saw 64 ICOs raise US$103 million. ICOs are attractive to entrepreneurs because they can be faster, less bureaucratic, and nondiluting, that is, startups issuing ICOs usually are not offering equity but rather a discount on the cryptocurrency. Of course, as the ICO space matures, experts are predicting ICOs will become more formalized and potentially regulated too. "A white paper and an 'about us' page will not be sufficient to raise $10m going forward" while ICOs "currently sit in the Wild West of financing."[15]

To date, venture capitalists have largely shied away from the ICO space. But they are starting to circle the wagons.

> Venture capitalists, who generally have been standoffish to the ICO phenomenon are now becoming more interested for a number of reasons. One is profits—cryptocurrency investors are making huge returns on not only Bitcoin and Ether but also emerging cryptocurrencies born from ICOs. Ethereum doubled in just a few days in March. Yes in three days, people who invested in Ether doubled their money. Some cryptocurrency investors are earning massive ROI in weeks and this fact is spinning heads.
> Liquidity is the second reason VC are interested. Rather than tying up vast amounts of funds in a startup or Unicorn and waiting for the long play—an IPO or acquisition—they can see gains quicker in ICOs and pull profits out easily.[15]

Blockchain Capital is one of the first venture capital firms really embracing the ICO model and in fact, raising their own funds for portfolio investments via their own ICOs with a token (coin) called BCAP. In their own words, Blockchain Capital is:

> a pioneer and the premier venture capital firm investing in Blockchain enabled technology companies. Our initial fund was the first VC Fund dedicated to the Bitcoin/Blockchain ecosystem, launched in the Fall of 2013, and was also the first fund to accept capital calls in Bitcoin. Based in San Francisco, Blockchain Capital invests in the best entrepreneurs who are fostering innovation in the Blockchain economy.[16]

CONCLUSION

As I have stated, and is clear from the last reference to Blockchain Capital, I do not actually believe venture capital will disappear anytime soon. As long as there are potentially scalable investment opportunities that could result in a fast exit, venture capitalists will be able to generate funds for investing in such projects. And, it is clear that even in the PCE world, there are startups operating on the border of traditional capitalist markets and post-capitalist markets, many of whom do aspire to become large, potentially even publicly traded, billion-dollar companies (or exits). Yet, the underlying values of those embracing PCE are different than billion-dollar exits. Entrepreneurs aspiring to create lasting value in their communities are frequently not pursuing ventures that are synergistic with the venture capital model. Furthermore, many projects like platform cooperatives and DAOs do not even offer easy mechanisms for venture capital investment. Instead, crowdfunding, ICOs, and even just embracing the efficiency of lean startup along with leveraging community assets (coworking spaces, fab labs, etc.) reduce the need for traditional startup financing for most PCEs. This leads to the next and final chapter of this book, where I will try to bring all of the concepts from this book, and other related post-capitalist topics like basic income, to explore how we could reimagine our economies at a local, city level.

REFERENCES

1. H. Neck, D. Meyer, B. Cohen and A. Corbett. 2004. An entrepreneurial system view of new venture creation. *Journal of Small Business Management* 42(2): 190–208.
2. B. Cohen, and P. Muñoz. *The Emergence of the Urban Entrepreneur: How the Growth of Cities and the Sharing Economy Are Driving a New Breed of Innovators*, Praeger, California, US.
3. P. Muñoz and B. Cohen. 2017. Towards a social-ecological understanding of sustainable venturing. *Journal of Business Venturing Insights* 7: 1–8.
4. Lily Rockwell, Author Dan Lyons Tackles 'Bro Culture' and Why it's Damaging to Tech Companies, 512Tech.com, March 2017, http://www.512tech.com/technology/author-dan-lyons-tackles-bro-culture-and-why-damaging-tech-companies/FUsdIKBesSvD7pCNGzPtsK/?utm_content=buffer2525a&utm_medium=social&utm_source=twitter.com&utm_ campaign=buffer. Accessed March 2017.
5. $77.3B in Total Venture Capital Invested in 2015, Report Finds, SSTI January 2016, http://ssti.org/blog/773b-total-venture-capital-invested-2015-report-finds-vc-trends-look-2016. Accessed September 2016.
6. Global Venture Capital Investment Market 2016-2020, Report Linker, July 2016, http://www.reportlinker.com/p03952883-summary/Global-Venture-Capital-Investment-Market.html. Accessed September 2016.
7. Steve Case, The Third Wave: An Entrepreneur's Vision of the Future, Simon & Schuster, New York, 2016.
8. Crowdfunding Industry Statistics 2015-2016, CrowdExpert 2016, http://crowdexpert.com/crowdfunding-industry-statistics/. Accessed January 2017.

9. Crowdfunding's Potential for the Developing World, InfoDev, World Bank Group, October 2013, http://www.infodev.org/crowdfunding. Accessed September 2016.

10. Startup Peerby Raises $2.2 million from users, Peerby, March 2016, http://press.peerby.com/125333-startup-peerby-raises-2-2-million-from-users. Accessed September 2016.

11. Alex Fortin, Cryptocurrency Opens up Venture Capital for Everyone, Alexfortin. com, March 2016, https://www.alexfortin.com/cryptocurrency-opens-up-venture-capital-for-everyone/. Accessed September 2016.

12. Coop Principal Investment Club thecp.coop December 2014, http://thecp.coop/wp-content/uploads/2014/12/Investment-Club-101.pdf. Accessed September 2016.

13. Private correspondence with Joe Riemann, co-founder of the Cooperative Principal.

14. Sid Kalla and Matt Chwierut, 2016: The Year Blockchain ICOs Disrupted Venture Capital, Coindesk, January 2017, http://www.coindesk.com/2016-ico-blockchain-replace-traditional-vc/. Accessed January 2017.

15. Based on working paper from Richard Kastelein with a working title *Tokenization in the age of blockchain*.

16. Blockchain.capital Homeage, http://blockchain.capital. Accessed March 2017.

7

Back to the Future

Around the world, a new economy is being shaped by a "leave things better" story about the meaning of progress and development. In a million projects, people are growing food, restoring soils and rivers, designing homes, generating energy, journeying, caring for each other, and learning, in new ways.

These activities are incredibly diverse, but a green thread connects them: the regeneration of local living economies. Growth, in this story, takes on a new meaning as the improved health of soils, rivers, plants, animals— and people. Production is re-imagined as a source of equipment for the local system: from greenhouses and water tanks, to solar panels and mesh networks.[1]

John Thackara
Author, How to Thrive in the Next Economy

What would happen if you merged all the new forms of post-capitalist entrepreneurship discussed in this book, with other alternative concepts not yet discussed in detail to reorient our economy in a way that works for all? I do not consider myself to be a futurist per se, and as such, I try not to spend time predicting the future. Instead, I observe emerging phenomena and try to connect the dots. In this chapter, my goal is to connect a lot of moving parts based on current initiatives around the globe which, when combined together, could dramatically alter our lives and society, while reshaping our thinking of entrepreneurship and entrepreneurial ecosystems. Thus, every suggestion in this chapter is actually happening somewhere in the world, although not together and not at scale, at least not yet.

WHAT IS THE RIGHT UNIT OF ANALYSIS FOR THIS FUTURE ECONOMY?

Of course, if we listened to a lot of the political rhetoric in the recent years, you might think the "back to the future" in this chapter's title might suggest that isolationist, nationalist models of economy reflect the future we should go back to. Instead, my view is that the most important territory for a future I want for my children is more urban and regional. This is not to suggest nation states and multilateral government actions will be irrelevant in the future. Yuval Noah Harari, the Israeli historian and best-selling author, has made strong arguments for the increasing importance of a global governance model, over national approaches, to address some of the world's most pressing problems such as climate change and income inequality.* The solid argument is that many of these issues are inextricably interconnected and require a collaborative effort from world governments. Sure, Iceland, New Zealand, Costa Rica, and Norway aim to be carbon neutral, but while more than a hundred other national governments refuse to make such bold commitments, we won't be able to meaningfully address climate change in time to avert further disaster. As Harari states, even with the concept of basic income (something to be discussed later in this chapter), there is a global interconnectivity in that automating jobs in Chinese factories for Apple means fewer jobs in China and also in the United States. Who is to pay the costs of basic income payments to US and Chinese factory workers?

Beyond the interconnected nature of complex challenges, in the 21st century, it is difficult to imagine a future where global connections could be cut off in lieu of a full return to local economic activity only. Web and blockchain technologies, addressed throughout this book, ensure that we are globally connected. Beyond digital connections, a return to almost exclusively local economies cannot be achieved for physical reasons either. Immigration will continue to happen, and as research has shown, that is actually good for local economies and entrepreneurship. Furthermore, some material resources do not exist in all societies which may be needed to help in a transition to a more sustainable society. Take the case of

---

* Harari had an interesting conversation about this topic and others related to this chapter in a 2017 TED Dialogues. https://www.ted.com/talks/yuval_noah_harari_nationalism_vs_globalism_the_new_political_divide

lithium which is a key input into batteries for electric vehicles and batteries powering many of our electronic devices. China and Chile combine to represent about 75% of global lithium reserves. If nations and cities wish to embrace electric vehicles, then they will be dependent on foreign inputs. And it probably doesn't make sense for every nation or region to build the capacity to make their own electric vehicles.

While the above all make the case for maintaining global connections, the shift back to increasingly local, but interconnected, economies is ongoing. In fact, I side with Benjamin Barber who has made a strong argument for a global governance structure made up of mayors instead of nationally elected presidents. Mayors have been taking a lead on a range of important issues including climate change and income inequality, often despite national policies to the contrary. Furthermore, innovation, as my friend Jeb Brugmann documented in his 2010 book,[2] increasingly diffuses from one city to another irrespective of national borders. Michael Porter, the famed strategy professor from Harvard Business School, was an early and frequent advocate of national innovation policy, before shifting toward regional clusters of innovation. Yet, several scholars and thinkers, such as urbanists Jane Jacobs and Richard Florida, have suggested that innovation and entrepreneurship policy should be explored from an urban perspective. With my 2016 book, I sought to continue that line of thinking by demonstrating how several factors are driving innovation and entrepreneurship into cities.[*]

I believe the right focus for a discussion of how post-capitalist entrepreneurship can thrive in a new reframing of the economy is local, primarily urban, while maintaining strong regional and global connections. So, the rest of this chapter will focus on how a city might combine all of the PCE models discussed throughout this book, along with other emerging policies and trends not yet discussed, to create an inclusive, sustainable economy for all its citizens.

---

[*] This paragraph seeks to summarize decades of thinking on innovation and entrepreneurship policy which of course is impossible to do in one paragraph. If you wish to read more on the evolution and debate regarding national versus regional versus urban innovation and entrepreneurship policy, Porter's *Wealth of Nations*, (1998); Jacobs' *Economy of Cities* (1970); Florida's *Rise of the Creative Class* (2002); and if you are so inclined, my book, *The Emergence of the Urban Entrepreneur* (2016).

POST-CAPITALIST ECONOMY

Almost unnoticed, in the niches and hollows of the market system, whole swathes of economic life are beginning to move to a different rhythm. Parallel currencies, time banks, cooperatives and self-managed spaces have proliferated, barely noticed by the economics profession, and often as a direct result of the shattering of old structures after the 2008 crisis. New forms of ownership, new forms of lending, new legal contracts: a whole business subculture has emerged over the past ten years, which the media has dubbed the "sharing economy." Buzzterms such as the "commons" and "peer-production" are thrown around, but few have bothered to ask what this means for capitalism itself. I believe it offers an escape route—but only if these microlevel projects are nurtured, promoted and protected by a massive change in what governments do. This must in turn be driven by a change in our thinking about technology, ownership and work itself. When we create the elements of the new system we should be able to say to ourselves and others: this is no longer my survival mechanism, my bolt-hole from the neoliberal world, this is a new way of living in the process of formation. (Paul Mason, *Post-capitalism: A Guide to Our Future*)[3]

While Mason's work has been criticized by many to be too Marxist, I believe the foundations of the arguments in *Post-capitalism* are quite valid, and this quote from the book briefly summarizes my goal for this book and, in particular, this chapter.

Local Governments and Post-Capitalism

In order for post-capitalist entrepreneurship to thrive at a local level, we will need local governments to create the enabling conditions. Local governments will need to rethink economic development policy, welfare policy, and citizen engagement strategies. I believe we will see cities increasingly shift away from entrepreneurship policies focused on encouraging job creation and tax revenues toward encouraging civic and post-capitalist entrepreneurship. First of all, fewer startups will be creating significant amounts of jobs in the future. As I discussed early in the book, technology changes will continue to drive job losses due to automation, robotics, artificial intelligence (AI), and big data. Furthermore, as Steve Case documented in *The Third Wave*, the overwhelming majority of startups in the future will never reach the scale of the platform capitalists which emerged at the end of the 20th century (e.g., Google, Facebook, Amazon).

Also, there is an increasing recognition from local governments that entrepreneurship policy and funding should support local entrepreneurs who will have an impact on the local community. This may occur via procurement for innovation projects like the program I helped lead for the Metropolitan Region of Santiago, Chile, whereby cities allocate a percentage of their annual budget to encourage innovative solutions to local problems, while at the same time, stimulating local, civic entrepreneurs to get a start. Citymart is a private platform that connects cities with entrepreneurs around the globe who have potential innovations for city challenges. Citymart has worked with more than 50 cities around the world to facilitate such connections by hosting challenges on their platform and assisting cities with the procurement process.

City governments will continue to develop entrepreneurship policies focused on post-capitalist entrepreneurship models. In 2012, the Mayor of Seoul, South Korea, launched a bold plan to become the world capital of the sharing economy. So far, they have succeeded too. Amsterdam has also been quite bold in its effort to collaborate with citizen groups and the startup community to bolster sharing economy activity. Barcelona has gone as far as to create a whole new line of activity within Barcelona Activa (the city's entrepreneurship agency) exclusively focused on promoting alternative economies. I have been working with this group almost since its inception in 2015. Led by Alvaro Porro, who was hired to direct these initiatives, the Alternative Economies group is focused on stimulating platform cooperatives and the circular economy through a combination of policy and funding support. One of their first tangible projects was the launch and support of La Comunificadora, which I discussed in Chapter 1, to support 15 sharing-economy startups, 13 of which were exploring platform cooperative and commons-based peer production models. Meanwhile, the city's CTO, Francesca Bria is envisioning driving grassroots transformations via digital social innovation (DSI).

Local Currency

Speaking of the role of local governments, there is clearly a role for cities to participate in supporting the growth of the local currency movement. While Colu, the Israeli startup supporting local digital currency initiatives discussed in Chapter 4, has often decided to initiate local currency projects without waiting for government support, other cities have been initiating their own local currency movements. There are more than 5,000 local currencies operating in communities around the world, many of which have direct support of the city governments. Paris, for example, made headlines in 2016 when they announced their intention to develop a local currency, Siene, to "encourage consumers and entrepreneurs to use local businesses and services, aiming to boost local employment and reduce environmental damage by transport."[4]

As I discussed in detail in Chapter 4, alternative currencies can be a source of stimulation of post-capitalist entrepreneurship, and of course the local nature of the currencies in many cases suggests that local currencies could form part of a transition toward a post-capitalist economy at a local level. Alternative currencies, not just digital currencies, but also timebanks, for example, facilitate a high velocity of transactions between local citizens and local producers. Local currencies could even be used as part of a universal basic income (UBI) or guaranteed minimum income (GMI).

Basic Income

It is highly unlikely that a future economy will create as many high- and medium-income jobs as our economy of the 20th century did. Capitalism has done a great job of creating wealth for the wealthy but has done a terrible job of supporting inclusive prosperity for all. This of course was the driver for the Occupy Movement, and arguably explains Brexit and Trump's rise to the Presidency of the United States, as well as the alt right movements that have gained steam in places like France and The Netherlands. People are frustrated that their quality of life does not appear to be improving and that the prospects for good jobs, even for the well-educated, appear to be in decline. The assumption that our contributions to society can be measured by how much you can make as a salaried or hourly employee of a company is a remnant from the industrial revolution. Before that, people contributed in a myriad of ways to their community and engaged in bartering and other models of value creation and exchange.

For centuries, scholars, policy makers, social activists, and elected officials have suggested that a basic income is a human right. The idea of a basic income is gaining a lot of traction around the globe as the reality that our current market economy is not creating inclusive prosperity, and instead is creating a growing precariat. Cities in The Netherlands, Finland, parts of Canada, Barcelona, and even Oakland are all engaging in some form of basic income experiments. Many basic income advocates insist that for a basic income system to work, it must be universal and unconditional. That is that citizens in communities and countries around the globe should be given a monthly income as a citizen of that community, without regard or expectation of contribution. The arguments for this form of UBI are solid. For example, individuals, especially women, in abusive relationships may feel more empowered to escape if they have certainty that a basic income would be provided unconditionally. An employee being paid minimum wage and being mistreated could leave her employer knowing an unconditional basic income is there to provide a floor. Note that in unconditional models of UBI, the payment is made monthly regardless of situation or circumstance or other income streams. So, under a classic UBI scheme, that employee working for minimum wage would also be receiving UBI payments simultaneously.

Alternative basic income models have been explored in recent years, including GMI. The difference with a GMI is that it may be conditional and can be offset by other income earned. This means that a minimum wage employee under a UBI scheme receives employment income and UBI payments regardless, whereas the very same employee in a GMI scheme may have the GMI payments reduced by the amount of income generated. In both cases, UBI and GMI, the incentive to work in minimum-wage jobs may be reduced. Yet, many argue that this is not an issue because over time, many such jobs will be automated.

I believe in a post-capitalist society, we will need to introduce a basic income model in some form to counteract the inequalities that have arisen in market economies. I am not convinced, however, that we will see full unconditional UBI implementation around the globe for a range of reasons. First, financing unconditional UBI to citizens around the world is no easy task. Furthermore, there will be significant political opposition in many countries to unconditional UBI as the cultural perception that people need to "work for a living" is persistent. Also, I believe some level of conditionality may actually be reasonable. For example, many UBI advocates suggest that basic income frees people to add value in society in their own way, which may include taking care of ill or aging family members. I agree. However, I believe that is just one example of the type of acceptable activity supported by basic income. I believe recipients of basic income should also be offered tools for getting back into the work force or, more likely, becoming a freelancer, active provider (and recipient) of timebanking services, or maker.

Basic income in some form will almost certainly be part of national policy in dozens if not all countries in the future. But also, I believe local governments may become active developers of basic income programs. In the United States, devolution of national powers to state and local powers has been a topic since Ronald Reagan's time in the Oval Office. As I articulated above, for many reasons, there is a growing focus on local governments and their ability to solve complex problems such as climate change and inequality. While some basic income regulations have been explored at a national level (e.g., the 2015 referendum in Switzerland), the basic income experiments are mostly happening at a local level.

The 2-year minimum income experiment starting at the end of 2017 in Barcelona suggests one direction for such a local model to basic income. In the Barcelona experiment, 1,000 low-income families will be given a fixed income over a 24-month period. Some recipients will receive the income unconditionally while others will have conditions, such as going through worker-retraining programs, in an effort to see how basic-income recipients behave under different program designs. But perhaps one of the most interesting components to the experiment in Barcelona is the development of a local digital, social currency which will represent a portion of the basic income payments for between 250 and 500 families. One of the ways we may be able to address a national government's perceived inability to finance a UBI program is to have some of the payments be made via local digital currency. Instead of paying US$1,000 per month to every citizen over the age of 18 at a federal level (the proposal by Andy Stern in *Raising the Floor)*, perhaps $600 is paid from the national government and $400 is paid in alternative local currencies managed by city governments. Interestingly, in the Barcelona experiment, the city aims to put conditions on the local currency including the requirement to apply some or all of the local currency toward the creation of a self-employment, social enterprise, and to work with local retailers and small businesses to accept the currency for items related to allowing the recipients to become self-employed.

In 2015, Grantcoin was launched as a blockchain-enabled alternative currency for the distribution of basic-income payments around the globe. In the first round, Grantcoin issued their digital currency to more than 1,100 applicants from 79 different countries. Grantcoin can currently be sent to others, via a pay-it-forward model, saved as an investment and even exchanged for Bitcoin. Of course, these uses do not pay for housing, food, and other basic needs, although in the future they hope to "persuade businesses to accept Grantcoin as a form of payment or as a coupon."[5]

Blockchain Cities

I have alluded to blockchain throughout this book, particularly in the chapter about digital currencies and the chapter on distributed autonomous organizations (DAOs). Distributed ledger technologies without a doubt pose disruptive and transformative potential and can become an important enabling technology for the transition to a post-capitalist society. Only recently the potential for blockchain to transform cities has started to draw attention from the blockchain community. On March 9, 2017, I was invited to attend the inaugural Blockchain Ecosystem Network (BECON) launch event for the Catalan chapter in Barcelona. Here, we had early conversations about what blockchain might mean for cities. BECON currently has an initiative called blockchain cities which

> is an initiative of BECON. The initiative is an EU membership platform of local authorities in BlockChain transition. Providing insights on BlockChain methodologies and solutions for cities—shaping urban services and products of the future.[6]

At the BECON event, Llluisa Marsal, who is helping to develop the Blockchain Cities initiative, suggested that blockchain could be the new code for cities, supporting urban codes, master planning, policies, and standards to meet sustainability challenges in cities. She also proposed that blockchain allows us to reimagine and reinvent our cities in a bottom-up, distributed and decentralized way.

We are in the very early days of what blockchain can mean for cities. Obviously, the smart cities movement with a strong focus on the Internet of Things (IoTs), big and open data, and sensor technology will likely benefit from the growth of blockchain solutions. But perhaps more interesting is to reflect on how blockchain could be used to support social inclusion and a post-capitalist society. Aside from its potentially transformative potential in local cryptocurrencies, blockchain may also support many other important changes to life and government in cities. As I discussed in previous chapters, the blockchain may support alternative forms of sharing economy that challenge platform capitalism. Take Arcade City as an example. It is a blockchain-enabled (with ethereum) organization aimed at taking on Uber first, and other platform capitalists later. It is a peer-to-peer app, founded in Austin, Texas, in 2016, which aids people seeking a ride with drivers of passenger vehicles. Unlike in Uber's model, Arcadian drivers are able to charge their own fees and process transactions directly with their passengers. Since its launch, rides have been facilitated in other cities in the United States, Europe, and Africa. Arcade City has launched their own initial coin offering in 2016, to create Arcade Tokens which can be used for payments with the app. Or similarly, we can look at Power Ledger, a startup in Perth, Australia, leveraging blockchain technology to allow:

> renewable energy asset owners to decide who they want to sell their surplus energy to and at what price. Using blockchain technology we provide a transparent, auditable and automated market trading and clearing mechanism for the benefit of producers and consumers. Our technology enables the sale of surplus renewable energy generated at residential and commercial developments (including multi-unit/multi-tenanted) and at homes and businesses connected to existing electricity distribution networks, or within micro-grids. Power Ledger puts the power to manage the energy economy into the hands of consumers, while maintaining the value of existing distribution networks.[7]

Blockchain could also have a big impact on how democracies operate at a local level. Many, myself included, have argued for the need to embrace continuous democracy in cities. Rather than vote once every 4 years (if that), technologies, including the blockchain, could be leveraged to facilitate frequent referendums of voters in online or mobile forums on initiative to improve their neighborhoods and their cities. The Institute for Technology & Society in Rio, Brazil, for instance, has built a blockchain-enabled voting tool that:

> will establish the identity of voters (based on a unique identification number each voter and taxpayer receives from the government in Brazil) and will allow them to formally express their support for social-driven draft bills.[8]

Similarly, interest in liquid democracy has been growing in recent years. The idea behind liquid democracy is that every citizen should have a say in the decisions made by government that will affect their daily lives. But instead of necessarily every citizen having to vote on every decision being made, under liquid democracy, a citizen could allocate their vote to specific citizen representatives over specific topics with citizens who share their values. Are you socially liberal and fiscally conservative? You could allocate your voting rights on social issues to someone who shares those values, while allocating voting rights on economic issues to someone who shares your conservative values. Yet, when a citizen feels particularly passionate and knowledgeable on other topics, he or she could choose to make a direct vote himself/herself, and even represent others who empower him or her to vote for them because he or she is an expert who shares their values on the topic. This combination of direct and indirect democracy gives rise to the concept of liquid democracy. Programmers working on ethereum and exploring liquid democracy through a DAO have even published a how-to-guide and shared the code for the mechanism to facilitate liquid democracy.[9]

Fab Cities

> Perhaps the greatest potential for change comes from the way the maker movement may alter urban landscapes, in terms of both community and spatial relationships. Economic and productive activity obviously plays a large role in urban development. With the growth of the maker movement, which views the consumer as producer, the biggest shift may come in the form of co-location of manufacturing, engineering, and design. The movement has the ability to draw production back into the cities where consumption occurs (resulting in) profound economic and social benefits. In addition to added jobs, proximity means more innovative potential for workers. The untapped skills and knowledge of out-of-work producers can become part of the creative economy of the city. (How Cities Can Grow the Maker Movement 2016)[10]

Throughout this book, particularly in Chapter 1 about commons-based peer production, I have made references to the emergence of maker spaces, and in particular, Fab Labs around the globe. At the time of writing, there were nearly 1,100 registered Fab Labs in cities in every region of the world. The Fab Lab concept of providing local citizen access to the tools of modern makers, like 3D printers, laser cutters, and CNC machines, and of course the maker community itself, has clearly resonated in cities around the globe. While I am a big believer in the maker movement and the Fab Lab community, I also have been reserved regarding its potential to, by itself, transform our global economy to one that is indeed more inclusive and more sustainable. In part, my reservations are with the recognition that many in society will never feel inclined or even capable of participating in this more high-tech maker movement. Over time, more open-source software and more designs are being shared with the global community, which make it easier for maker neophytes to participate. The emergence of the Fab Market as a virtual marketplace for accessing proven designs for downloading and printing using local materials at any Fab Lab in the world is a promising development as well.

Yet, the promise of the Fab Lab concept, which is to offer space for makers to come together and to experiment with making products with local materials, is broader than just the Fab Lab itself. Key members of the Fab Lab community, including Tomas Diez, referenced earlier in this book, recognize the real power of the Fab Lab model as a more holistic resource for local productive systems that has ignited a new movement within the Fab Labs community: Fab Cities. The audacious goal of cities who sign up to be part of the Fab Cities movement is to produce at least 50% of everything consumed in the city within the city by 2054, without dependence on importing products from foreign lands. Sixteen cities have signed up for this commitment, including Amsterdam, Barcelona, Boston, Detroit, Santiago, and Shenzhen. Also, the newly formed Fab City group has developed a proposal for 7 million (euros) to pilot the Fab City concept, with a particular focus on how the Fab City model could enable a circular economy. The cities committed to participating in the program include Amsterdam, Barcelona, Berlin, Copenhagen, Ioannina, London, Milano, Paris, and Zurich.

> There is a pressing need to reimagine cities and how they operate in order to respond to the ecological and social challenges of our time. Cities hold the potential for the reinvention of the current linear economy paradigm to a Circular Economy, and the Fab City Prototypes project aims to accelerate this paradigm change, allowing consumers to become actors of the design, prototyping and production processes at the local scale, while sharing knowledge globally. We build on the premise that individual change is essential to catalyse a collective transition towards more sustainable lifestyles. In this regard, citizens need to engage in self-transformation—which can be enabled through new product cultures and new cultures of design and production. The immediate outcome of the project will establish the necessary urban frameworks and lighthouses to guide policy makers to scale the results to metropolitan and bioregional levels. This will be fostered by partnerships with industry and local authorities. Linking micro-enterprise and citizen-led spaces with corporate and government sectors will create an ideal test ground to develop and implement approaches for an inclusive and impactful Circular Economy. The ambition is to pave the way for locally productive and globally connected cities, that foster social cohesion and well-being. (Proposal entitled Fab City Prototypes)

Thankfully, we do not have to wait for that project to hopefully get funded and completed to see an early example of what a Fab City model could look like. Tomas Diez, together with the Mayor of Barcelona, Ada Calau, and other leaders of the alternative economy movement in Barcelona have come together to support the creation of the Maker District of Poblenou. Poblenou is an old industrial part of Barcelona which, in 2001, was converted into one of the world's first urban innovation districts.[3] As a member of the Board of Advisors for the Fab City project, and in context of this book, I sat down with Diez in March 2017 to discuss where the Fab City concept could go and how it could overlap with other topics covered in this book and in particular this chapter.

Diez noted that when we talk about the blockchain, redistribution of manufacturing, and local food production, they all seem to stay at an abstract level because there is a disconnect between the idea and the implementation. Within the Fab City team, there are more than 60 people thinking about how to create experimentation areas in neighborhoods to test the ideas and ground them in urban realities. Diez suggested that cities need to embrace experimentation and really encourage grassroots maker projects. Further he recoomends cities create special development zones at city scale in which you prototype different approaches, for example, a neighborhood with an orientation toward supporting cooperativism, perhaps digital neighborhoods embracing blockchain and DAOs while others could be like maker communities, etc. This is not that different than what I experienced when I lived in Buenos Aires several years ago. Inspired by Barcelona's own 22@ innovation district, the then Mayor of Buenos Aires, now President of Argentina, Maruicio Macri, encouraged the creation of seven different clusters loosely located in neighborhoods which already had a critical mass of community assets oriented toward those themes, including technology district, design district, arts districts, and a fashion district.

Diez views Fab Cities as a multiscalar model treating the city as an ecosystem bringing energy, food, and products closer to where they are consumed. Diez belives that in the next 20 years, it is reasonable to believe that the average citizens will have 3D printers in their home to allow them to repair or make basic household items, while Fab Labs may exist in several neighborhoods to serve not only as spaces for prototyping new product and innovation ideas but also as a community resource for aspiring makers and students to learn and interact with others. Finally, he believes that many cities will have some form of flexible factory based on industry 4.0

(i.e., robotics) that will operate similarly to a Tesla factory but will be flexible enough to:

> produce skateboards one day, shoes another day and cellphones the day after. Users could be part of fabrication process.[11]

Three-dimensional printing technology is advancing very rapidly and some 3D printers are even capable of reproducing themselves, so it is easy to foresee a time when 3D printers become more ubiquitous, meeting Diez's first level of the future Fab City. The second level, of having Fab Labs in cities around the globe, is definitely underway with more than 1,100 already not including the thousands of maker spaces not certified as Fab Labs. While the third level may seem more futuristic, that of flexible factories based on industry 4.0 available at the city level to produce products in larger quantities for local consumption, even this reality is already here. The Innovative Manufacturing Engineering Systems Competence Centre, founded in Tallinn, Estonia, in 2009 is financed by Enterprise Estonia and the EU Regional Development Fund. Based on flexible manufacturing and industry 4.0, the center aims to:

> improve the competitiveness of Estonian engineering industry and to develop cultural, ethical, and social values based on increasing integrated industrial use of new technologies of optimal product life-cycle management (PLM) and e-manufacturing, emerging manufacturing technologies and process automation techniques, and new forms of self-organizing systems with online monitoring and diagnostics in order to gain competitive advantages and assure economic success in a global economy, to rise the effective use of knowledge in product engineering and manufacturing planning for small series production in distributed and networked organizations of Estonian engineering industry.[12]

Diez is an urban optimist but admits there are many challenges to achieving this future from who will own and operate the flexible factories (with what business models) and how can we avoid letting the robots rule the world. He is also concerned about the maker cities framing in the United States which seems dominated by a neoliberal view of how the private sector can monetize makers and turn them into venture-capital-backed startups. In contrast, the goals for Fab Cities are to address social exclusion from our current market economy and diminish the ecological impact of our current productive system. Furthermore, the hope of Fab Cities is to actually make formal Fab Labs obsolete by supporting the transition to embedding the maker ethos across society and all sectors from no-tech to architecture and the blockchain.

██████████████

LOCAL LIVING ECONOMIES

A focus on living systems means a new kind of infrastructure. New kinds of enterprise are needed: food co-ops, community kitchens, neighborhood dining, edible gardens, and food distribution platforms. New sites of social creativity are needed: craft breweries, bake houses, productive gardens, cargo bike hubs, maker spaces, recycling centers, and the like. Business support is needed for platform co-ops that enable shelter, transportation, food, mobility, water, elder care to be provided collaboratively—and in which value is shared fairly among the people who make them valuable. Technology has an important role to play as the infrastructure needed for these new social relationships to flourish. Mobile devices and the Internet of Things make it easier for local groups to share equipment and common space, or manage trust in decentralised ways.[13]

Local Food Production

Let's talk food in a post-capitalist society. Obviously, food is a necessary ingredient for life. But beyond that, it is also a powerful reflection of local cultures. Yet, as has been well documented, much of our global food system has not only lost its connection to local cultures, but it has also brought disease and chemicals into our food supply and contributed to climate change among other ills.[4]

> When people succeed in profiting on a large scale, they succeed for themselves. When they fail, they fail for many others, sometimes for us all. A large failure is worse than a small one, and this has the sound of an axiom, but how many believe it? Consolidation and conglomeration have created a Big Food world that is so pervasive and so powerful. When it fails, the results are tragic and epidemic.[14] (Wendell Berry)

Resistance to the global food system has been growing in the past few decades with a range of initiatives, including the growth of organic food markets, increased interest in farmers' markets (e.g., there was a 180% increase in farmers' markets in the United States from 2006 to 2014[15]), and a range of new business models, such as that of SPUD introduced in Chapter 1 or Brighter Farms who operates a network of localized, aquaponics facilities for distributing to grocery stores (including some-times even operating on the roofs of the supermarkets themselves!).

> A positive cause, still little noticed by high officials and the media, is the by now well-established effort to build or rebuild local economies, starting with economies of food. This effort to connect cities with their surrounding rural landscapes has the advantage of being both attractive and necessary. It rests exactly upon the recognition of human limits and the necessity of human scale. Its purpose, to the extent possible, is to bring producers and consumers, causes and effects, back within the bounds of neighborhood, which is to say the effective reach of imagination, sympathy, affection, and all else that neighborhood implies. An economy genuinely local and neigh-borly offers to localities a measure of security that they cannot derive from a national or a global economy controlled by people who, by principle, have no local commitment. (Wendell Berry)

Referring back to the idea of Fab Cities and makers for food, recall the case of Aquapioneers discussed in Chapter 1. Started by international founders in Barcelona's Green Fab Lab, their solution allows local resi-dents and restaurants to print their own closed-loop aquaponics solution for local food production and consumption. Entrepreneurs have also been developing 3D printers capable of printing foods with locally sourced ingredients. Meanwhile, in Minneapolis, the Lakewinds Food Co-op has created the Maker-to-Market incubator to support cooperative food start-ups. The Maker-to-Market program not only provides entrepreneurial support for aspiring food entrepreneurs but also offers access to a shared commercial kitchen and shelf space in Lakewinds retail outlets.

Local Energy Production

Earlier in this chapter, I referenced Power Ledger who is aiming to democ-ratize renewable energy production and distribution among peers, lever-aging blockchain technology. This is but one of thousands of initiatives around the globe seeking to localize and democratize such a powerful and essential resource in more sustainable and inclusive ways. The Portland, Oregon-based, nonprofit group, EcoDistricts has been pioneering new models for neighborhood-scale energy and sustainable community strat-egies for the better part of a decade. Portland itself has been a pioneer, with five separate ecodistricts throughout the city. While each ecodistrict in Portland, and around the world, vary significantly in focus, they are all neighborhood-scale sustainability initiatives and most of them have locally produced, renewable energy as a key part of their strategy.

I have personally had the pleasure to have some involvement with a few such projects, such as the Dockside Green project in Victoria, Canada, which has a biomass to energy solution and the Athletes' Village in Vancouver which leverages waste heat from the sewer system to heat the neighborhood. Speaking of waste heat to energy, Copenhagen has managed to supply 97% of the city's heating needs with waste heat recovery.[16] In Vienna, the city collaborated with the local energy company to offer Citizens' Solar, a crowdfunding investment opportunity for local residents interested in helping the city meet its renewable energy targets through the development of solar projects throughout the city. Meanwhile, in Warwick, UK, the Midcounties Co-operative launched Co-Operative Energy in 2010 to compete with the six big, for-profit energy producers. Citizen groups, cooperatives, neighborhood associations, and PCEs around the globe are continuing to experiment with alternative approaches to finance, generate, and distribute more local, more renewable energy sources than what the for-profit energy grid operators offer.

CONCLUSION

I realize this final chapter may feel futuristic to some, while lacking details to others. My goal with this chapter was to advance the conversation regarding the potential to ground post-capitalism at a territorial level, in this case, cities. I believe cities represent the convergence of idealism, innovation, entrepreneurship, and a sustainability ethos, and have the most potential to make PCE a reality. However, it is important not to lose sight of the increasing interconnected, global nature of society as resource flows and migration do not stop at artificial territorial boundaries. And, of course, many PCE solutions discussed throughout this book, and indeed even in this chapter, are digital and by their nature somewhat without boundary, such as Bitnation's Decentralized Borderless Voluntary Nation (Chapter 5) as well as most other DAOs and even platform cooperatives. But if we are to transform our economy to something that is inclusive and sustainable, we must look to our cities where the vast majority of citizens live, and where we have the levers, and the citizen engagement, to rethink our economy from the ground up. While, like Tomas Diez, I consider myself an urban optimist, I do not believe we will see the complete elimination of neoliberal capitalism in cities around the globe. Instead, I believe post-capitalism, and the PCEs I have highlighted throughout this book, will compete with and even sometimes collaborate with traditional market enterprises. Hopefully, the profit-driven enterprises of the future will at least embrace the values of the benefit corporation movement such as the numerous B Corps I highlighted in Chapter 2.

I suspect in the future, at least the future I hope to see, we will witness cities embracing everything from local digital currencies, three-tiered maker communities (in the home, in the neighborhoods, and city-level flexible manufacturing production), some form of basic income (perhaps tied to civic contributions), hopefully affordable housing for all through community land trusts and other housing innovations (e.g., Vancouver's in-fill housing), blockchain-enabled distributed sharing platforms that compete with, or maybe even replace, platform capitalists, entrepreneurial and maker education in all schools and accessible to adult residents, and significant amount of civic crowd-funded projects. What I am certain of is that new forms of commons-based, open entrepreneurship, enabled by technology, and grounded in interconnected local communities is here to stay and will transform our cities and our lives.

REFERENCES

1. John Thackara blog post, February 27, 2017, http://thackara.com/development-design/making-as-reconnecting-crafts-in-the-next-economy/. Accessed March 2017.
2. J. Brugmann, 2010. *Welcome to the Urban Revolution*, Bloomsbury Press,
3. Paul Mason, *Postcapitalism: A Guide to Our Future*, Macmillan, London, UK, 2016.
4. Tony Cross, Paris Considers Launch of Local Currency, RFI September 2016, http://en.rfi.fr/economy/20160904-paris-considers-launch-local-currency. Accessed October 2016.
5. Grantcoin homepage, http://www.grantcoin.org/use-grantcoin/wallets/twitter/. Accessed March 2017.
6. Becon Global Hompeage, http://www.becon.global/blockchain-cities/. Accessed March 2017.
7. Powerledger.io homepage, https://powerledger.io. Accessed March 2017.
8. Ronaldo Lemos, *Using the Blockchain for the Public Interest, Medium*, October 2016, https://medium.com/positive-returns/using-the-blockchain-for-the-public-inter-est-2ed1f5114036#.b5slsdq12. Accessed February 2017.
9. How to Build a Democracy on the Blockchain, Ethereum.org, https://www.ethereum.org/dao. Accessed March 2017.

10. Brooks Rainwater, *How Cities Can Grow the Maker Movement, National League of Cities*, Washington, D.C. 2016.

11. *Private conversation with Tomas Diez*, March 16, 2017

12. IMECC Linkedin Homepage https://www.linkedin.com/company-beta/2021106/?pathWildcard=2021106. Accessed February 2017.

13. John Thackara, Manifesto for Utopias are Over: Cities are Living Systems, P2P Foundation, March 2017, https://blog.p2pfoundation.net/manifesto-for-utopias-are-over-cities-are-living-systems/2017/03/14. Accessed March 2017.

14. Cynthia Belliveau, What's Wrong with our Food System, UVM.edu, May 2012, https://learn.uvm.edu/foodsystemsblog/2012/05/21/whats-wrong-with-our-food-system/, Accessed February 2017.

15. Luke Runyon, Are Farmers Market Sales Peaking? That Might be Good for Farmers, February 2015, http://www.npr.org/sections/thesalt/2015/02/05/384058943/are-farmer-market-sales-peaking-that-might-be-good-for-farmers. Accessed February 2017.

16. Case Study: Copenhagen, c40.org, November 2011, http://www.c40.org/case_studies/98-of-copenhagen-city-heating-supplied-by-waste-heat. Accessed January 2017.

Appendix: The Logic of the Commons and the Market

	The For-Profit Paradigm	The Commons Paradigm
Resources	• Scarcity is given or created (through barriers and exclusions).	• For rivalrous resources, there is enough for all through sharing. • For nonrivalrous resources, there is abundance.
	• Strategy: "Efficient" resource allocation.	• Strategy: Strengthening social relations is decisive for assuring fair shares and sustainable use of resources.
Idea of the individual	• Individuals maximize benefits for themselves (Homo economicus).	• Humans are primarily cooperative social beings.
Human relationships to nature and other humans	• Separation • Either/or • Individualism versus collectivism • Human society versus nature	• Interrelationality • Individuals and the collective are nested within each other and are mutually reinforcing.
Change agents	• Powerful political lobbies, interest groups and institutionalized, politics focused on government.	• Diverse communities working as distributed networks, with solutions coming from the margins.
Focus	• Market exchange and growth (GDP) achieved through individual initiative, innovation, and "efficiency."	• Use-value, common wealth, sustainable livelihoods, and complementarity of enterprise.
Core question	• What can be sold and bought?	• What do I/we need to live?
GOVERNANCE		
Decision-making	• Hierarchical, top-down; command and control	• Horizontal, decentralized, bottom-up. Self-organization, monitoring, and adjustment of resource use.
Decision principle	• Majority rules.	• Consensus.

SOCIAL RELATIONSHIP		
Power relation tendency	• Centralization and monopoly.	• Decentralization and collaboration.
Property relations	• Exclusive private property. "I can do what I want with what is mine."	• Collectively used possession. "I am co-responsible for what I co-use."
Access to rival resources (land, water, forest)	• Limited access; rules defined by owner.	• Limited access; rules defined by users.
Access to nonrival resources (ideas, code...)	• Limited access; scarcity is artificially created through law and technology.	• Unlimited access; open access is the default norm.
Use rights	• Granted by owner (or not). Focus on individual rights.	• Co-decided by coproducing users. Focus on fairness, access for all.
Social practice	• Prevail at the expense of others; competition dominates.	• Commoning; cooperation dominates.
KNOWLEDGE PRODUCTION		
	• Corporate ideology and values integrated into education and knowledge production.	• Peer-to-peer, networking, and collaboration allow diversity of viewpoints.
	• Knowledge regarded as scarce asset to be bought and sold.	• Knowledge regarded as plentiful resource for the common good of society.
	• Proprietary technologies.	• Free- and open-source technologies.
	• Highly specialized knowledge and expertise are privileged.	• Knowledge is subject to social and democratic control.
IMPLICATIONS FOR		
Resources	• Depletion/exploitation. Enclosure.	• Conservation/maintenance. Reproduction and expansion.
Society	• Individual appropriation versus collective interests. • Exclusion.	• "My personal unfolding is a condition for the development of others, and vice-versa." • Emancipation through convivial connections.

Creative Commons Share a Like, Silke Helfrich

Index